The Magick of
Chant-O-Matics

The Magick of Chant-O-Matics

Raymond Buckland

REWARD BOOKS

Library of Congress Cataloging-in-Publication Data

Buckland, Raymond.
    The magick of chant-o-matics.
    ISBN 0-13-545079-9, ISBN 0-7352-0374-1
    1. Success.   2. Incantations.   I. Title.
BJ1611.2.B79   1978   77-13984
131'.32—dc20   CIP

ISBN 0-7352-0374-1

REWARD BOOKS

www.penguin.com

146119709

WHAT THIS BOOK
WILL DO FOR YOU

*E*nvy! The dictionary says that envy is "a feeling of discontent and resentment aroused by another's desirable possessions or qualities, with a strong desire to have them for yourself." Do you envy others . . . or do others envy you?

There is no reason in the world why you should not be the object of others' envy. Have you ever wanted things for yourself? Good health? Love? Money? A constant, steady income, or a sudden inheritance; a lottery win, or a discovery of treasure? Perhaps your desires are for less material things—a true love; the healing of an unhappy marriage; regained health; protection from evil? Or perhaps you wish to control others; to have them do your bidding? All these things can be yours. All these things are within your grasp. All these things can make you the envy of others.

This book reveals the secrets of gaining your own personal desires. Not through hard, time-consuming, constant exercises and gradual development over many months, but through simple, easy-to-do rituals that are a joy to perform.

NEARLY THREE HUNDRED DIFFERENT CHANTS FOR ALL POSSIBLE NEEDS AND DESIRES

Nearly three hundred different chants are included in this book. Chants that, when properly used as directed, will bring you that which you most desire—that which will truly make you the envy of others. Chants for Money; chants for Power; chants for Health; chants for Protection.

For a quarter of a century I have studied the many aspects of the Occult. For years I have taught psychic development in universities, colleges, at adult-education classes, and to private students. Through all this time I have come to realize one important thing in particular— that anything you desire can be yours . . . anything!

MAGICIANS OF THE PAST

The Magicians of the Middle Ages strove mightily to gain their desires. They conjured spirits, commanding them in complex esoteric terms and called upon God and the Angels to aid them in their efforts. Their rites were long and complicated. Frequently they had to spend months in preparation. Yet all this preparation could be for naught if one small item was overlooked, or one small tool not properly prepared.

With this book the intricacies of the Ceremonial Magicians can be thrust forever into the background. With no preparation, with the simplest of "tools" (e.g., candles and incense), you can immediately obtain that for which they struggled for so long.

CHANT IS POWER

Prayer is universal. Every religion throughout the world, in all places, at all times, uses prayer. In many religions the prayers are chanted. Psalms are a form of chanted prayer. What is the purpose of the chant? How does it affect the prayer?

The chant, it turns out, is the key to successful prayer. Why? Because it puts you into the prayer!

The chant is a form, a style, a method of approach that ensures the drawing-off of your own personal "power" (or mana) from within and, through it, projecting your desires.

Don't be afraid of the word "prayer"! You want a certain horse to win the 3:30 race? In wanting it to win you are, in effect (or in reality), praying for it to win! To go to the dictionary again, prayer is "a reverent petition made to a deity or other object of worship." This does not mean you have to be religious, in the strict sense of the word, in order to pray. After all, at the race-track you might be praying to the great God Luck! . . . or to his brother the God of Gambling!

But to want, or even to literally pray, for your horse to win may not be enough. You need the personal factor.

Frank C. was an inveterate gambler. He especially liked to play the horses—even though he invariably lost!

"Why do you keep pouring your money down the drain this way?" I once asked him.

"Well, odds are that one day I'm bound to win!" he grinned.

I started telling Frank a little of what I had learned over the years about getting what you desire.

"It's not enough to stand at the rail and scream for your horse to win," I said. "The gods help those who help themselves. Why not put some of your own power behind your horse? You push him to the front, ahead of all the others."

"With my mind?" he asked, incredulously.

"Certainly," I said. I went on to explain a little of how a simple chant can act as a catalyst, and draw out the power that lies dormant within all of us. I even wrote down for him a chant designed specifically to bring about a gambling win (see Chapter 2). By the time I had finished a strange gleam had come into his eyes.

GAMBLING CHANT BRINGS $5,000 WINNINGS TO FRANK C.

Turning to his racing-sheet he moved his finger quickly down the list of runners in the next day's races. Expertly he checked off with his pencil the ones he fancied. "These are the ones I'm going to work on," he said smugly.

I didn't see Frank for a week or two after that, but the next time I did see him he was driving a brand new car.

"What happened to your old 'bomb'?" I asked.

He grinned. "Gave it away," he said. "I bought this with my recent winnings on the horses. I won over $5,000 in ten days! You were right, you know. It's the personal touch that makes the difference!!"

CHANT WORKS AUTOMATICALLY

The steps to achieving your desires are simple and straightforward. By following the steps given in this book, for using the nearly three hundred different chants, attainment is automatic! For that reason I label it CHANT-O-MATICS. Decide what it is you want. Follow the simple ritual, using the chant to draw out your personal power, and the results follow naturally. It's as simple as that.

Five different chants are given for each objective. All are equally effective, so you can choose whichever you prefer, whichever you feel most comfortable saying.

HOW MUCH TIME MUST YOU DEVOTE TO CHANT-O-MATICS?

Forget the weeks of preparation. Forget the months of study. Forget the days of ritual. Granted you can acquire nothing by the single wave of a "magic wand," but there is no need to go to the other extreme like the magicians of old. As I told Frank C., "the gods help those who help themselves." You must expect, then, to put a little effort into getting what you want. That effort, however, need take no more than a half-hour of your time! In some cases the Chants need to be repeated at regular intervals, as will be later detailed, but many of them are "one-timers" only.

HOW DEIDRE C. USED A SIMPLE MARRIAGE-SAVING CHANT TO TURN NEAR-DISASTER INTO A SECOND HONEYMOON

Deidre C.'s marriage was going on the rocks. There seemed no way she and her husband could be brought back together again. But Chant-O-Matics worked where family, friends, marriage counselors, and clergy failed. Within two days of doing a simple five-minute chant, Deidre was packing her bags for a second honeymoon with the husband she adored (see Chapter 10).

Deidre C. need not be alone in changing her luck—and her life—for the better. YOU can influence the forces that be. YOU can lay out the map of your life and follow sure-footed along the roads you plan.

THE TIDAL-WAVE OF MONEY THAT THREATENED TO SWAMP ERIC S.

Chant-O-Matics work in all areas of life. One of the areas where there is, perhaps, greatest need is the financial. Yet here it is equally efficacious as elsewhere. Take the example of Eric S. (Chapter 3). An old man, Eric S. was in the awkward position of having money—but having it "tied up" so that he could not make use of it for the everyday business of living. Almost to the point of starving, Eric S. turned to a time-tested chant to bring him financial gain. Overnight the Wheel-of-Fortune turned full circle! Eric was embarrassed with the sudden influx of wealth! He had more money than he could handle—and every minute brought him more!

YOUR POWER UNLOCKED

Remember, the chant is merely a tool used to unlock your power; to bring out the kinetic energy within you and start it rolling towards your personal goals. You have the power; Chant-O-Matics merely lets you make use of it.

Raymond Buckland

CONTENTS

HEALTH

Part Five
PROTECTION

PART ONE

PREPARATION

1

YOUR CHANT-O-MATIC WORKSHOP

One of the first requirements for the Magicians of medieval times was a room in which to work. For them, however, it could not be just any room. The *grimoires*—old books of magic—were most specific in what they said about the requirements for such a magical workroom. For example, *The Book of Sacred Magic of Abra-Melin the Mage*, written in 1458, says:

> Ye shall choose an Apartment which hath a Window, joined unto which shall be an uncovered Terrace (or Balcony), and a Lodge (or small room) covered with a roof, but so that there may be on every side windows whence you may be able to see in every direction, and whence you may enter into the Oratory. In which place the Evil Spirits shall be able to appear, since they cannot appear within the

Oratory itself. In which place, beside the Oratory towards the quarter of the North, you shall have a roofed or covered Lodge, in which and from whence one may be able to see the Oratory. . . . The Oratory should always be clear and clean swept, and the flooring should be of wood, of white pine; in fine this place should be so well and carefully prepared, that one may judge it to be a place destined unto prayer.

The Terrace and the contiguous Lodge where we are to invoke the Spirits we should cover with river sand to the depth of two fingers at the least . . . and if one maketh his Oratory in desert places, he should build (the Altar) of stones which have never been worked or hewn, or even touched by the hammer . . . .

THE JOY OF SIMPLICITY

Happily you do not have to do anything so elaborate to practice Chant-O-Matics. Simplicity is the keynote.

Everything you use may be of the simplest. You are not going to be conjuring Spirits, evil or otherwise, so you do not need any Circles of Protection, nor Northern outer Lodges adjoining your Oratory. You do not need to cover your floor with sand, nor even to ensure that your floorboards are of white pine!

LOCATION

Although Chant-O-Matics may be done anywhere, at any time, it would be preferable for you always to use one particular room. This can be your bedroom, your living room, your kitchen, or wherever. If you have a spare room—perhaps in the attic or basement—then this would be better, but it is by no means mandatory.

If you have a choice of rooms available, then pick the room that will be quietest. If you live on a busy road, then a room at the rear of the house, away from the traffic noise, would be best. The size of the room is unimportant since you will be using only a small area in it.

You need the room to yourself when working, and you should feel happy in your mind that while you are in it you will be free from any interruptions.

FURNISHING YOUR WORKSHOP

The main item of furniture is your "Altar." This can be made specifically for the purpose, or it can be adapted. A small card table, a coffee table, the top of a chest of drawers, will do fine. Size is not critical.

Cover your Altar with a white cloth and, in the center, stand an incense-burner. The incense you use can be church-type incense sprinkled over glowing charcoal, or can be of the simple "cone" type available in dime stores. If you use the church type (which is more economical), but do not have a suitable censer, fill a dish with sand and stand the charcoal on that. The sand will then absorb the heat and prevent scorching of the table.

At the start of each individual chant, a particular incense might be recommended. For example, when seeking love it is traditional to burn a mixture of Saffron and Pepperwort. If you have access to these particular items, then by all means use them. Certainly they are "traditional." However, if you cannot obtain what is recommended, then substitute any pleasant-smelling incense. It will not negate the ritual.

On either side of the censer, toward the rear of the Altar, stand a tall, white candle. If you would like to include a religious figure or picture in the Altar set-up, then stand it between two candles, behind the censer. Lay this Chant-O-Matic book in front of the censer and your Altar is complete.

The height of your Altar will dictate whether you stand, sit, or kneel for your Chant-O-Matic rituals. Whichever you do, there is no reason why you should not be comfortable. If you are to kneel, then why not position a cushion or some other kneeling-pad on the floor before the Altar?

DRESS IS YOUR OWN INDIVIDUAL THING

When doing the simple Chant-O-Matic rituals, it is important that you feel comfortable. In this way you can best concentrate on what you are doing, and concentration is important. To this end, then, dress comfortably.

When many Witches perform their rituals and work magic, they work naked, claiming that the absence of clothing leaves them completely free and unrestricted, not only in body, but also in mind and spirit. You may wish to do your Chant-O-Matics in this manner.

Ceremonial Magicians, on the other hand, wear elaborate robes, frequently decorated with intricate magical designs. For them, these robes are of a purely utilitarian nature. Again, you may wish to emulate the Magicians. Certainly, for some, the wearing of special clothes helps induce the right mood for the rituals.

But there are those who feel most comfortable, no matter what they are doing, in their "everyday" clothes. Perhaps a particular baggy sweater and faded jeans; a worn house-coat; a favorite dress; or just whatever happens to be handy! The choice is yours.

How Cheryl W. Used Chant-O-Matics to Obtain a Chant-O-Matic Workshop!

▶ Cheryl W. was a student of mine who became very enthused on learning of Chant-O-Matics.

"My problem," she said, "will be in finding somewhere to do the rituals."

I told her what I have already told you—that a small area in any room will suffice.

"But that doesn't help," complained Cheryl. "You see, I have only a small one-room apartment—and I share it with a roommate! She is always there when I am and she would think me crazy, and probably keep interrupting, if I tried to do my Chant-O-Matics with her present."

We pondered this problem for a while. Then, as a temporary measure, and to give Cheryl an opportunity to "test" Chant-O-Matics, I offered the use of a room in my house for a while.

"The very first time I use it," she said with a grin, "will probably be the last. You see I've decided to work first of all toward getting my own Chant-O-Matic workshop!"

Her words turned out to be prophetic: She used my room just once. She did the chant "to bring pressure to bear on another" (see Chapter 9). The "other" she had in mind was her landlady, thinking that only through her could extra room become available.

Sure enough, within 24 hours of Cheryl doing the chant, her landlady offered her the use of a small spare room just along the passageway from her apartment!

"I just got rid of some old trunks I had stored there," said Mrs. M., "and thought perhaps you girls would like to put some of your things in there. . . . Give yourselves a bit more elbow-room."

Cheryl thanked her and, mentally, thanked Chant-O-Matics. The room was small, but ideal for use as a private Chant-O-Matic workshop.

TIMING OF CHANTS

When is it best to do Chant-O-Matics?

A time of day when you can be quiet and free from interruption is best. For some people this means early morning; for others, it is afternoon; for still others, late evening. Whichever is best for you, is best.

If you are doing Chant-O-Matics regularly, then try always to do them at approximately the same time of day each time. This way you will find it easier to get into the right frame of mind for the ritual.

Some chants especially benefit by being performed on a certain day. For example, Love chants should always be done on a Friday; Money chants should be done on a Wednesday; Protective chants on a Saturday (these beneficial days are given, where necessary, at the start of the individual chants in the following pages).

If you cannot do your Chant-O-Matic on the day suggested, then do it on the closest day to it that you can manage. The correct day will certainly give an added "boost'" but who knows, perhaps your desire is strong enough to overcome any change of day?

LENGTH OF CHANTS AND YOUR "POWER"

Some chants are long; others are short and repetitious. The length of the chant has no bearing on its effectiveness. Most of the nearly three hundred chants in this book—whether short or long—have the same basic meter; a sort of "dum-de-dum-de-dum-de-dum" rhythm. It is this rhythm that draws out your power and sends it on its way.

I have known people who use a small drum, or bongos, to emphasize this beat . . . and very effectively. I have known others who, having learned the words by heart, would dance around the Altar in a circle, again to emphasize the beat.

You can do this. Anything you feel will help draw on your desire, and send it pounding through the air to its goal, can and should be used. Don't feel self-conscious. In fact this is why I suggest that you practice Chant-O-Matics alone. Then if you suddenly feel like dancing, or singing, or beating your hands on your thighs, or whatever, you can do so! Get *involved* with the chant. As I said in my introduction, the chant is merely a tool used to unlock your power; to bring out the kinetic energy within you and start it rolling toward your personal goals.

CHOOSING—AND "TAKING AIM"

Choose carefully to get the right chant for the right job. Think about what you want *exactly*. For example, suppose the girl you want is in love with another . . . don't rush off and do the chant "to separate a couple" (Chapter 8). After all, they may well separate—but then she may go off with someone else, not even noticing you in the interim! Better by far, then, to start with the chant "to win the love of the one you desire." Once you have that she will automatically drop the other guy!

Having decided on the right chant, be very careful "taking aim!" You want some money? Decide whether you want to win the state lottery *or* to win the daily double. Both would be nice, but if your mind is dithering between the two, your directed power will equally dither—and perhaps miss both! So decide which it is to be, aim carefully, and pull the Chant-O-Matic trigger!

This is especially important, of course, when you are dealing with people . . . be it for love, health, protection, or anything else. In fact, when working for a particular person, it night will help your concentration to have a photograph of the subject lying on the Altar, for reference.

WORKING FOR OTHERS

There is no need to be selfish with Chant-O-Matics. Use the chants for yourself by all means. But use them for others too. There are many people in this world desperately in need of help. Some need money, yes, but many more need health, love and companionship. *You* can provide much of this through Chant-O-Matics. And from helping others you will find you help yourself.

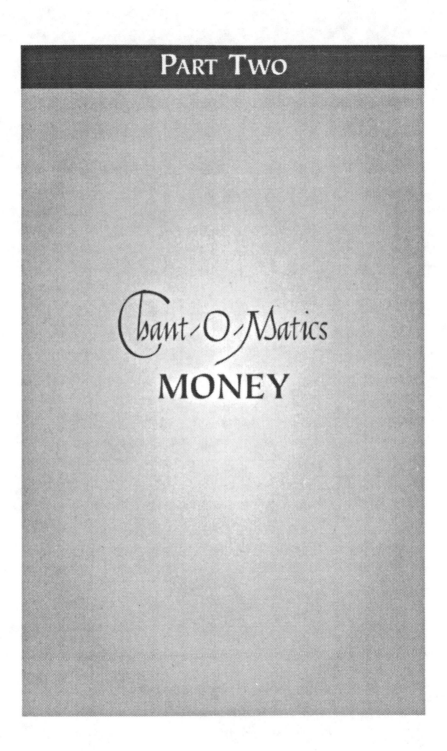

PART TWO

Chant-O-Matics
MONEY

2

MAGIC MONEY CHANTS THAT CAN PUT YOU KNEE-DEEP IN THOUSAND-DOLLAR BILLS

*T*he vast majority of people are content to live on a moderate income. So long as they can meet their bills, have the occasional night out on the town, and keep pace with the people next door, they are content. This is good, and as it should be.

Yet even the average person meets face-to-face with a crisis once in a while. The burst water-heater; the leaky roof; the orthodontic work; the need for an extension on the house, etc, How to find the large sum of money suddenly required? Up to now this has been a problem—a very real headache. But now, with Chant-O-Matics, you can breathe a sigh of relief!

Once in a (very long) while it seems you get an unexpected financial windfall. Perhaps it's a tax refund, or an unlooked-for inheritance, or the horse you splurged five dollars on comes in at 100 to 1! These events are certainly cause for celebration, but why do they never coincide with the crises?

Where was that winning outsider when your wife got the bill for her root-canal work? Where was the overtime check when the maple tree fell on the garage? Where was your late dear Uncle George's two-thousand-dollar legacy when you had to add the dormer? In the general run of life, the two never seem to get together. Yet now, with Chant-O-Matics, you can *bring* them together!

You can see to it that whatever problems come up in your life, however much money you suddenly find yourself in need of, you have the power to cover the emergency. Through Chant-O-Matics you can be master of any situation. That crisis that would knock your neighbor to the ground will not even cause you to stagger!

Chant-O-Matics will not only cover your financial crises, and leave you smiling, it will also give you such an air of confidence, of self-assurance, that even your closest friends will notice a change in your outlook on life. You will be looked to as the one they can always count on.

ODDS AGAINST WINNING

The odds against your winning any of the greater games of chance are staggering. With state lotteries, for example, they are many thousand to one. The odds against you can be ignored, however, when you practice Chant-O-Matics. There is no way to measure the effect that your personal power can have on a horse race, a lottery drawing, or especially something so seemingly unaffected as an inheritance. Through chant you can not only reduce the odds against you but you can actually *reverse* the order, and end up with odds in your favor!

By utilizing any one of the 15 chants given in this chapter, you can bring to yourself sudden wealth sufficient to cover any emergency. Whatever your financial need, you can meet it. Remember, though, that you are only to seek what you *need* . . . if you want money just for the sake of having it, it is unlikely to work!

DECIDE ON A METHOD

First consider your need. How much money do you actually require? Sit down with a pencil and paper, if necessary, and work it out. Now, what would be the ideal way of meeting that need? If you are a gambler, then a win on the horses, or at cards, or whatever your particular bent would seem to be indicated. You don't gamble? Then perhaps you would prefer an inheritance or something similar? As a writer I usually think in terms of an unexpected royalty check from one or other of my publishers. You might think along those lines.

When you have decided on the way you would like the money to come, *stick with that decision,* and choose one of the chants, on the following pages of this chapter, appropriate for that choice.

FIVE CHANTS FOR A FINANCIAL WINDFALL (*e.g., inheritance*)

It is preferable that this chant be done on a Wednesday.

Light your candles and incense (suggested incense: a mixture of Pepperwort, Saffron, and Nutmeg).

Sit for a moment and think hard about the *exact* amount of money you need. *See* the money. See yourself holding it; counting it. Imagine not that it *will* come, but that it *has* come—that you now have it. With this in mind, you may start the chant.

Try to think of the words, of what you say, as you chant them. Get the rhythm so that it is automatic. Sit, stand, or kneel; whichever is most comfortable. You may use any one of the five following chants:

1 Suddenly I see the pile,
   Suddenly I hold the sum,
   Suddenly I end my trial,
   For the money—it has come!

   For the money that I need,
   For the need that is so strong,

For those words that I do read
Brings the money right along.

Brings the money without waiting,
Brings the money right to me,
Brings the answer to my waiting,
Suddenly I will be free.

Look hard into the smoke of the incense and, again, see the money in your hands. Again chant:

For the money that I need,
For the need that is so strong,
For those words that I do read
Brings the money right along.

Brings the money without waiting,
Brings the answer right to me,
Brings the answer to my waiting,
Suddenly I will be free.

Close your eyes, place your finger tips on your temples, and again see the money in your possession. After a few moments of this visualization, open your eyes again and chant:

Suddenly I see the pile,
Suddenly I hold the sum,
Suddenly I end my trial,
For the money—it has come!

2 Need, need, need;
Money, money, money!
Me, me, me;
Money, money, money!
Now, now, now;
Money, money, money!
Need, need, need;
Money, money, money!
Me, me, me;
Money, money, money!
Now, now, now;
Money, money, money!
Bring the money to fill the need;
Yes, bring the money to fill the need.
Now my power has done the deed!

3 Out of the nowhere,
Out of the air;
Out of the darkness
To aid me, I swear.
Pile upon pile
Of silver, of gold;
Come without warning
As you have been told!

4 Stream into river.
River into sea;

Let the rivers of money
Flow straight through to me.
Swift is the current
And fast is the flow;
So let all my coffers
With gold overflow!

5 Like a flash of lightning bright,
Stabbing suddenly down to earth;
Let the money that I need
Come to me, yes, give it birth!
Money, money—silver, gold;
Pouring, rushing, piling high,
All I want to meet my needs
Will come to me, yes, by and by.

FIVE CHANTS FOR A GAMBLING WIN (e.g., *lottery, racing, cards*)

This chant can be done on any day of the week.

Light your candles and incense (suggested incense: a mixture of Mastic and Frankincense).

Sit for a moment and think of the approximate amount of money you need. *See* the money. See yourself winning it. See it coming to you.

Sit, stand, or kneel—whichever is most comfortable—and chant. You may use any one of the following five chants:

1 Gods that rule Luck, may you smile down on me!
All that I wager may come back times three.
The roll of the dice, or the turn of the card,
Be it carefully watched so that winning's not hard.

Gods that ride Luck, may you increase my gain.
See that my bets are not placed there in vain.
Increase my winnings and make me the one
Whose balance of chance now is tipp'd to be won.

2 Run the horse and turn the card,
Spin the wheel—to win's not hard!
Roll the dice, or what you will,
Luck my way will ever spill.

Though I bet what e'er I own,
The winner I shall be alone,
Run the home and turn the card,
Spin the wheel—to win's not hard!

3 Winning, winning, winning state;
Spinning, spinning, spinning fate;
Betting, letting, getting gold;
Mounting, counting, gabbing hold;
Yes, all the winnings I can hold.

4 Double, treble, ten times, o'er,
Money piled on money more.
What I bet will multiply.

What e'er I gamble, satisfy,
Racing, cards, or spin of wheel,
All will help the coffer fill.
Double, treble, ten times o'er.
Money piled on money more.

5 The Gods of Chance smile down on me,
The Wheel of Fortune spins, you see,
To win I cannot fail, I know.
The gold and silver start to flow
Into my hands, it cannot stop
Until I've gathered all the crop.

In each of the above chants, repeat the chant twice more, making three times in all. Then sit quietly for three or four minutes with your eyes closed, seeing yourself in your mind, winning at whatever you chose: cards, horses, dice—anything you want to work big in your favor.

FIVE CHANTS FOR SUDDEN EARNED WEALTH *(e.g., tax refund, overtime pay, etc.)*

It is preferable that this chant be done on a Wednesday.

Light your candles and incense (suggested incense: a mixture of Pepperwort, Saffron, and Nutmeg).

Sit for a moment and imagine you are holding a check in your hands. See yourself looking at it. See it made out for the exact amount you need. With this in mind, start the chant (any one of the five below). While chanting, try to actually feel the check in your hands, between your fingers.

1   Hard I worked and labored long,
Mindful that my power was strong.
In the past this deed was done;
I harvest now the prize I won!

2   Here is the wealth I earned in the past,
Come to reward him who needs it at last.
Rich the rewards so long ago won,
Forgotten but lost not, returned; it is done!

3   Though great is the need
And long was the wait,
The Gods they take heed
And temper the Fate.
The money long earned
Now comes through to me,
I never was spurned
For the prize now I see.

4   I never ask for unearned aid,
Only for what I know was made
By me, in time that long passed by.
Now there's a need, so to me fly
With all haste, that I may pay
My debts, and settle all this day.

5 Earned long ago,
To me now flow.
Do not delay.
I need it this day.
Silver and gold,
Money to hold;
Answer my needs
With rewards for my deeds.
Earned long ago,
May it to me now flow.

Say the chant five times in all. Each time chant it a little faster and a little more forcibly, so that by the fifth and last time you are almost shouting it. You will *feel* the power flowing out of you; you will *feel* the energy you have built up.

How Nancy J. Brought an Unexpected Inheritance to Her Father

▶ Nancy's father was self-employed. He worked hard and he worked long hours, but somehow, it seemed he was never able to build up that little extra nest egg that he wanted to store away in case of emergencies. Nancy knew that her mother was worried by the way her father drove himself. Relentlessly he worked, hardly ever taking a day off to rest and relax. It seemed inevitable that he would eventually collapse from over-exertion.

A vacation was the obvious answer, but without that nest egg to tide them over, such rest and relaxation was out of the question. Day-by-day Nancy watched her father sink lower and lower. Dark circles surrounded his eyes; his shoulders sagged. Still he drove himself relentlessly on.

Nancy had been practicing Chant-O-Matics for several months. She had attended some of my classes and found that chants definitely helped her in many things. However, she had never attempted chants for any major situation. Now, it seemed, was an opportune time to begin. Choosing the chant "for a financial windfall," Nancy put her whole mind and energy into it

Two days later, Nancy's father received a letter from a law firm. The letter mentioned the will of his late aunt. He had known that she had died; that had been almost six months before. What he hadn't known was that she had died a relatively wealthy woman. Her estate had finally been settled and the money divided up among her many nephews and nieces. Nancy's father was to receive almost three thousand dollars! The nest egg had arrived!

How "Chief" Burr Won $11,250 When He Most Needed It

▶ George Burr was a Chief Technician of the Bomber Command of the British Royal Air Force. He was known affectionately as "Chief" to the men under him in the radar-servicing unit. Chief Burr was a basically simple man, not seeking super-luxuries for himself or his family. The one thing he did want, however, more than anything else, was a house of his own. He and his wife and children lived in the married quarters provided at the base. In such circumstances he was, in effect, regulated 24 hours a day. Service regulations governed the color of his house, both outside and in. If he wished to erect a simple tool-shed he had to "go through the necessary (lengthy) channels." Structural alterations, should he wish to make any, were out of the question! Chief Burr's pay was such that he could never hope to save enough money for a down payment on a home of his own, much as he would love one.

Not a gambling man, generally, Chief Burr did contribute a dollar a week to the unit's Football Pool. In Britain there is an extremely popular system of gambling based on guessing the number of drawn games in the results of each week's football (soccer) calendar. In the Chief's unit there were one or two "experts" who worked out the possible combinations and filled out the forms. Then a total of 20 people—Chief Burr included—put a dollar each into the pool, planning to divide equally any resultant winnings.

The pool had operated for over a year without a win, yet the contributors—and especially the "experts"—were ever hopeful!

One day, Chief Burr read an article of mine on Chant-O-Matics and, on the spur of the moment, did the chant "for a gambling win." Imagine his surprise when, that week, the Radar Servicing Unit won 225,000 pounds among them! At long last Chief Burr was able to buy a house of his own.

How Widow W. Saved Her Home from Foreclosure with a "Windfall" Chant

► Old Mrs. W.'s husband had died two years ago. He had carried little life insurance and the widow was hard-pressed to make ends meet. By doing odd jobs of sewing she was able to keep food on the table, but her mortgage payments on the small cottage fell further and further behind.

It seemed she was destined to lose the home she had known and loved, with her late husband, for so many years. She was desperate. What could be done? The bank was on the point of foreclosing on the mortgage.

One day, quite by chance, her neighbor—for whom the widow did some sewing—mentioned the power of Chant-O-Matics. The neighbor was an old student of mine.

"Try it," said the neighbor. "There is one, for a financial windfall, that is absolutely right for your situation."

The widow promised she would, but inwardly she doubted that anything could save her.

On her way home she spent one of her hard-earned dollars on a state lottery ticket. Then, hurrying home, she went straight to her bedroom, set up a simple altar, and read the chant from the piece of paper her neighbor had written it on.

For the next few days she felt guilty that she had spent the dollar, thinking her situation hopeless. Imagine her surprise when, at the next drawing of the lottery, she won $10,000!

3

INCREDIBLE CHANTS
TO INCREASE
YOUR INCOME

KEEPING PACE WITH THE
RISING COST OF LIVING

Inflation! Inflation! The cry is ever-present, and the evidence cannot be ignored. Prices are skyrocketing in all areas. It seems never ending. The housewife is especially conscious of the upward-spiraling food bill. What to do? How to keep pace with such mercurial costs? It's a question of trying to take three steps forward just to stay in the same place!

Yet those "three steps forward" can be taken with Chant-O-Matics! Through simple rhythmic intonation, it is possible to keep up with yourself.

IT IS POSSIBLE FOR YOU TO MOVE UP IN THE WORLD

Not only is it possible to keep up, but it is even possible to *overtake* yourself! Let others worry about their budgets and their bills; you can be making headway. There is no reason at all why these inflationary times should retard your economic growth. As others fall behind, you can be moving steadily forward. You can even pass those you used to see far ahead in the distance. By following your choice of one of the 15 chants given in this chapter, you can take yourself and your family onward and upward to bigger and better things. Once again, nothing is impossible.

NO DESIRE IS TOO GREAT FOR YOU

There are several ways of improving your lot. Whichever you choose can be the right way for you. For example, are you happy in your present job? Ask yourself, and examine the situation thoroughly. If you are, fine. Stay in it—but give yourself a raise! Yes, you give yourself a raise . . . through Chant-O-Matics.

If after careful consideration, however, you realize you are not too crazy about your present job, then get yourself a better one—"better" both in terms of happiness in the job *and* in terms of higher pay. Again, make the change through Chant-O-Matics.

There are other ways to improve your lot besides through your job situation, of course—increasing your income through receiving interest on investments, for example. For many this might be the ideal way. Once again this can be achieved, very simply, through chant. Decide which is the way for you, and go to it. Just follow the simple instructions on the next few pages and become one of the "lucky" ones who prosper.

FIVE CHANTS FOR A RAISE

This chant may be done any day of the week.

Light your candles and incense (any pleasant-smelling incense).

Sit for a moment and decide *exactly* how much of a raise you wish to receive. Concentrate on that amount. See yourself with a paycheck in your hand and *see* the new total on it.

Sit, stand, or kneel—whichever is most comfortable. Start the chant (any one of the below five may be used):

1 The workman is worthy of his hire,
Who works right through and does not tire.
When at week's end he takes his pay,
His *just* reward for every day
In his, without the need to plead

For recompense to match his deed.
So henceforth let the record show
That all is well; that all is so.

Again concentrate and see the amount on the paycheck in your hand.

2 Rising upward to the height
Of what I know is fair and right.
Leaving all the past below,
Going high and leaving low.
My reward for work well done
Shows the battle has been won!

Repeat twice more (three times in all).

3 Breaking free,
Moving high;
Aiming up
Toward the sky.
Floating, soaring,
Ever on.
Days of want are now all gone.
Better, better,
Pay by far,
To take me up
Toward the stars.

4 As bubbles spring up from the depth of the well
And burst on the surface, their presence to tell;
So up from the depths of the world all around
Do I spring to announce that I am not bound
By the chains that drag down all those that do fear;
No, I am the Master—myself I do steer.
And whate'er I want then it shall be mine;
I'll eat of the best, and I'll drink of the wine!

The following is an ancient magical chant, possibly ancient Arabic. Its exact meaning and origin have been lost in the passage of time.

5 Aye ab, abber abra;
Kah! Brakad!
Kad, kadder, kaddab.
Dabbar, dabbar, Kadabbar!

Each of the above should be said three times in all (in the case of #5, *five times* in all). Between each chant get a clear picture in your mind of the paycheck or pay envelope, bearing the new, increased wage.

FIVE CHANTS FOR INVESTMENT, OR OTHER INTEREST

It is preferable that this chant be done on a Wednesday.

Light your candles and incense (any pleasant-smelling incense). Sit, stand, or kneel—whichever is most comfortable—and chant. You may use any of the following five chants:

1   From the seed that I plant doth grow the big tree;
Its size in no time makes its origin wee.
It covers so soon an incredible space.
Uplifting its boughs; to the sun shows its face.
As the tree grows from seed,
As it springs up so high,
Let my interest grow
On the investments I buy!

2   Higher and higher, growing so big.
With never a pause as each shoot and twig
Enlarges the size of the main branch and bough,
That in turn will double and treble my vow.
Whatever the seed, wherever I plant,
I know that my harvest will never be scant
Whatever the seed, wherever it's planted,
I know that my wishes will always be granted.

3   Grow, show, go!
Earn, earn, return!
Go, allow, grow!
Return, yearn, earn!
However little; however much;
What was a little will grow at the touch
of the life, of the luck;

with courage, with pluck.
Grow, show, go!
Earn, yearn, return!
Go, show, grow!
Return, yearn, earn!

4 The winds carry the little leaf
To heights it never done could reach.
It soars ever upward with no way to slow
The rate at which its height doth grow.
Higher and higher, without even trying;
No thought of returning and no fear of dying.
From humble beginnings to heights never dreamed;
Increase without effort, for so it is deemed.

5 See it growing, see it increasing!
See it growing, see it increasing!
See it growing, see it increasing!
Onward and upward let the total grow;
Multiply like a rolling ball of snow.
Doubling, then trebling; bigger than big.
No matter how much of the profits I dig,
The source remains constant and generates more.
I know that I never again will be poor!
See it growing, yes, see it increasing!
Oh, see it growing; see it increasing!

FIVE CHANTS FOR A BETTER JOB

These chants can be done on any day of the week. Light
your candles and incense (any pleasant-smelling incense).

Sit, stand, or kneel—whichever is the most comfortable—and chant any one of the following:

1   Better by far, in every way.
Better my job so let me not stay.
Onward I go, to much better pay.
So let me enjoy this position.

Better and better as day passes day,
Better and better in every way.
This job I seek, Oh, with it may
I continue to enjoy this condition.

Better in money, and hours of the day;
Better in making me happy and gay.
Whatever the change I know that it may
Greatly improve my position.

2   I leave the old,
I greet the new.
I leave the fold
Of the stagnant crew.
To better live
To better sup,
To myself I give;
I move on up.

3   A change is for the better,
And never for the worse.
So as I speak each letter
I know I break the curse

Of stagnant job and lowly pay,
of wretchedness for me.
I know I move, from day to day,
Until success I see.

4 Cumana, chumana, banana, bee;
Semana, demana, lemma, mee.
Squaballa, baballa, raballa, roo;
Timana, vimana, wimana, woo!

To be said six times in all. (Old English "nonsense" chant is not so nonsensical when it proves effective!)

5 From chrysalis to butterfly
The change is very certain.
My change of job, though not so high,
Will be the opening curtain.

A better job with better pay,
The hours will be less wearing.
No matter how they shape the day
I will be better faring.

How Bob M. Got Three Better Job Offers in One Day After Doing a Five-minute Chant!

▶ Young Bob M. worked for an airline. It was a good job, but to Bob's mind, it didn't pay enough. He had recently left his parents' home to take an apartment alone, and he was feeling the strain of supporting himself. He had over-extended himself in all directions and the only solution he knew was to get a better-paying job.

Bob started the slow, laborious route toward his goal by enrolling for evening classes to improve his qualifications. One evening, quite by chance, he sat at the same table with me, in the college cafeteria, having a coffee before class. We fell into conversation and he found that I was teaching a course in Chant-O-Matics. In no time at all he decided that mine was the faster route to achieve his goal. I let him sit in on my class that night and he assiduously took notes.

It wasn't long before Bob felt ready to do the chant for his situation *(Chant for a Better Job)*. The following day he hadn't been at work for more than half an hour before he got a phone call. A friend had heard he was looking for another job and was calling to tell him of an opening where he (the friend) worked. The job was a good one and the pay was better than in Bob's present position! He had hardly put down the phone when a co-worker came in to tell him of another job position, again much better than his present one. Later that day, yet a third position became known to him!

How Jim P. Was Given Unexpected Promotion the First Time He Used Chant-O-Matics

▶   Jim P. was an avid stereo-enthusiast. All his money went into new equipment—bigger and better speakers, headphones, and CDs. He would frequently go without food in order to put the money toward some new stereo item. Consequently when his dentist suddenly informed him of the need for extensive dental work, Jim had no reserve funds to cover the lengthy treatment.

The only solution to cover both the monthly payments on his stereo equipment *and* the weekly dental work seemed to be a better-paying job, or promotion in his present one. The latter seemed highly unlikely since Jim had only been with the firm for three months. It was a good firm and Jim enjoyed working there. He was, therefore, loath to go seeking another job, though that seemed the only solution.

One day, in the midst of his dilemma, Jim chanced to read an article on Chant-O-Matics in a magazine at his dentist's office. It was one of a series of articles and Jim wrote away for copies of the others in the series. A ray of hope seemed to gleam for him. Though not entirely convinced of Chant-O-Matic's effectiveness, Jim hopefully did the chant for a raise. Within two days he was startled to be summoned to his boss's office.

"An unexpected situation has developed," said his boss. "Your immediate supervisor—Tom—has given us his notice. It seems he has some family problems that cannot be resolved. Although you have only been with us a relatively short time, we feel, on Tom's recommendation, that you are the right man to take over his position. Naturally, an increase in pay goes with the job."

How Impoverished Eric S. Brought on a Tidal Wave of Money that Threatened to Swamp Him!

▶ Eric S. had carefully planned his future—or so he thought. He had taken any spare money, over the years, and invested it in a wide variety of interests. He felt sure that when he reached retirement, he would be able to sit back and live comfortably off the interest. Unfortunately, it did not work out that way.

When Eric retired, it seemed that all his holdings were down; all his investments were doing little more than holding their own. Eric was therefore in the frustrating position of, in effect, having money but being almost penniless. He let bills pile up in the hope that there would be a sudden reversal of luck, but nothing happened. Things were beginning to look desperate when Eric found Chant-O-Matics.

There was no food on the table, no heat in the house, and no great will to live on Eric's part, when he finally followed the advice of a long-time friend and did a chant to bring interest from his investments. He really had no faith in the power of the chant, but was willing to grasp at any straw.

He was amazed when, without warning, his stocks began to soar. Not just one or two, but dozens of them! He suddenly found he was a rich man . . . and the money didn't stop! Day after day he got news of new advancements. He had more money than he would ever need, but still it did not stop. And that was how it continued, with no more worries for Eric S.

4

CHANT YOUR WAY
TO A CONSTANT
FLOW OF MONEY

*T*he country's economy is a dynamic thing—its ups and downs have us all riding the merry-go-round of inflation, deflation, stagflation, or other forces with fancy names. If massive layoffs or unemployment don't exist, they always seem to be lurking in the shadows. In this atmosphere of uncertainty, rather than seek job advancement and increases in paychecks, many are more than happy to settle simply for job security. To know a paycheck—whatever its size—will keep coming in, week after week, is all the security they ask. A *constant*, rather than a rising, income is the goal of many people today.

LAYOFFS AND FREQUENT UNEMPLOYMENT CAN BE LEFT BEHIND

Many people follow a stepping-stone existence. They get a job, work for a while, and are then laid off. They step to the next job. Again they work for a short while, but again they get laid off. On they go, stepping from one job to another, like following an irregular line of stones across a stream.

Some people miss their footing! They flounder about in the stream as the current buffets them against the unseen obstacles, Finally they struggle up onto another stone—only to continue their erratic progress, ever in fear of falling. How nice to sit permanently on a large island in that stream, secure in the knowledge that you do not have to keep moving.

NO NEED FOR YOU TO DRIFT AND WORRY FROM WEEK TO WEEK

There are also the drifters. Perhaps not as desperate as the stone-steppers, the drifters really lead no better existence. They drift from job to job, many times leaving one of their own volition only to curse themselves when they find no other opening awaiting them. But both types have a common feeling—worry! Worry about how to pay bills. Worry about the rent, the mortgage, putting food on the table and gas in the car. Worry!

Now, thanks to Chant-O-Matics, worry need not be a part of YOUR life. A simple chant, chosen from the ten in this chapter, will bring you the job security you seek. A constant income can be yours. Oil will appear to smooth the troubled waters of any current friction, and a steady job—with its income—will be yours!

FIVE CHANTS TO KEEP STEADY JOB

These chants can be done on any day of the week.

Light your candles and incense (any pleasant-smelling incense).

Sit, stand, or kneel, whichever is most comfortable.

1 No more worry,
No more fear,
No more thinking
Where to go from here.
No more doubts
Of how to keep
My job, I have
No need to weep.
A steady job
Will now be mine.
I know my future
Now is fine.

2 Flame without flickering
Burns strong and true.
Shielded from high winds
That blustered and blew.
No matter the danger
That 'round me may blow,
I know of my job
I will never let go.
It never will vary
And I will remain
Employed and well-paid,
And enjoying my gain.

3 Today and tomorrow,
And day after day;
I continue my work
I take home my pay.
While others may worry
About how to last
In their jobs, I do know
My security's fast
Today and tomorrow.
And day after day:
I'll continue to work.
I'll keep drawing my pay!

4 Should all the worries in the world
Be poured upon my head,

'Til could neither sit nor stand,
But wished that I was dead.
Yet still I know that all were naught
And I could still survive,
For while I have my job
I know that I am safe.

5 Up left, down left,
Steady left, –hold!
Up right, down right,
Steady right, –hold!
Forward, rear, above, below;
All of these I know are so.
Fast and firm
Held so firm.
Tied in place;
Cannot turn free.
Steady, steady,
Steady, hold!

FIVE CHANTS TO SETTLE A JOB SITUATION

These chants can be done any day of the week.

Light your candles and incense (any pleasant-smelling incense).

Sit, stand, or kneel, whichever is most comfortable.

(Chant each word/line three times, holding the sound as long as you can and concentrating your thoughts on a settled job situation.)

1 Ommm ...
Lummm ...
Shemmin ...
Thrommm ...
Stammm ...
Bemmm ...
Hommm ...

2 The forces that swing me
To left and to right.
Are now being centered
Till all is held tight
No more will I wander
And wonder what will,
For now I do know
My position is still.
As all that is held firm
Will settle at last,
So now can I count on
My turns being past.
All is at peace now,
And all is at rest;
From henceforth I know that
I will have the best!

3 The clamor of the battle
Die slowly from the day,
And phantom figures fighting

Are seen to fade away.
The mists do swirl about them
And cover them with gray,
Till I am left done at last
To do just what I may.
Alone and undisturbed I am,
And that is all I pray.

4 The rolling of the waves does tend
To swing the boat around,
Until the helmsman, though he tries,
His true course can't be found.
He fights the force of sea and wind,
He struggles vainly on.
Yet useless is that struggle for
The forces drive him ill.
When all is calm and all is smooth
No struggle does ensue,
For calm, still waters all around
Will give to him his due.
And as such calm will heal his wounds,
And make life good and grand;
So will that settling influence
Bring ME all that I planned.

5 Rocks and boulders strewn around
Everywhere, about the ground.
Without stumbling, where to turn?

How am I ever going to learn?
Yet so easy can it be
To dear that earth and let me see
The way, the way that leads aright
To settling down, to life, to might.

How Gordon H. Got a Good, Steady Job, "Against All the Odds"

▶ Gordon H. was not young. He had led a somewhat precarious existence, drifting in and out of jobs in several different cities. At almost 50 years of age, with a wife and three children to support, it seemed unlikely that he would find another good job when the company for which he worked unexpectedly went out of business. Age is not supposed to be a consideration when potential employers are interviewing applicants for job openings. It was not altogether surprising to Gordon, however, when he found that it always seemed to be the younger men who got the jobs. He became despondent.

One day he came home early from his round of the employment agencies, and sat forlornly watching a daytime talk-show on television. I happened to be one of the guests on that show and I expounded on Chant-O-Matics. Gordon was only half listening to what was said, but his wife absorbed it all. She later wrote to me, care of the television station. She explained her husband's position and implored me to help him. In replying, I told her that he could easily help himself, with

Chant-O-Matics. I enclosed a copy of the chant *To Bring a Steady Job.* In Gordon's dejected state it didn't take his wife long to convince him that he should at least give the chant a try. He did so.

The next morning Gordon went after a job as manager at a supermarket. There were several other men there for interviews. Most of them were younger than Gordon, and many had experience in the field. I was not surprised to hear later from his wife that it was Gordon who got the job!

How Beryl L. Ended a Succession of Layoffs Through a Simple "Settling" Chant

▶   It seemed that no sooner did Beryl L. get back into the swing of her work than she was laid-off again. Unemployment was common in the New England area where she lived, so she felt herself lucky for the few short weeks that she did get work But it was unsettling, to say the least, and it meant she could never quite catch up with the backlog of bills that accumulated. The factory where she worked so sporadically was the only one in the town and, with forever rising costs, the management could only bring in the evening shift—Beryl's—for short periods at a time.

Beryl watched her pile of unpaid bills grow and grow. She received a weekly unemployment check, but it did not fulfill a budget based on her original full-time earnings. She managed to keep food on the table, but it was a struggle even to do that. It was to help take her mind off her problems that one evening she sat down to read a magazine. It did not particularly hold her interest until she came upon an article on Chant-O-Matics. Avidly she absorbed all that it said.

Later that evening she was all set to do her chant. What could be more appropriate, she thought, than the example given in the article: the chant to settle a job situation?

The next morning she received a call back to work. A big order, with a promise of future ones, had come in and all shifts were needed. There was no indication that there would be any more layoffs for a long time to come.

5

SETTLE YOUR DEBTS
WITH A CHANT

*T*he height of frustration is when you have a sudden need for a certain amount of money; you don't have the money, but that amount is owed to you by somebody else! Perhaps you lent a friend $200 when he needed it, and you happened to have it available. He was obviously grateful and promised faithfully to repay you in six months' time. Six months later you need that $200, but the friend just can't come up with the money after all. What can you do?

YOU DON'T NEED
COLLECTION AGENCIES!

Frustrating as it may be, it need not signal the end of what has obviously been a good friendship. Circumstances change. If he was a good enough friend for you to have lent him that amount of money in the first place, then you can rest assured that there is good reason—and anguish on his part—that he cannot repay it. You don't need to resort to collection agencies, or any other legal tactics, to get it back. Rather, *help* your friend so that he may repay you. How to help him? Through Chant-O-Matics.

NEVER FEAR TO LEND
TO A FRIEND IN NEED

Whether the amount lent be $200, $2,000, or only $2, the point remains the same. You have a need now, and he has an obligation to repay which he cannot fulfill. This is not an uncommon situation among friends, but that doesn't make it one that should dissuade you from ever lending anything to someone close and in need. Lend, which you are able, with good heart. Most times you will receive back the loan with no problems. But when there *is* a problem, let Chant-O-Matics take over.

YOUR GUARANTEE
OF REPAYMENT

Chant-O-Matics is, in effect, your own personal guarantee that what you lend will be repaid. There are most effective chants (given below) that ensure the repayment of any debt. It works in a variety of ways. To some it may bring an unexpected windfall; to others, a better-paying job; to still others, perhaps, discovery of long-forgotten treasures. How it works on the other party is really of no concern to you. All that matters is that you may rest content in the knowledge that it *will* work in some way for him. He will suddenly find himself in the position of being able to repay what he owes.

Should it not be a *friend* who cannot repay you, the chant is equally effective. Perhaps someone owes you money and, for whatever reason, *refuses* to pay. It may even be that you have taken legal steps to ensure the return of your money. Whatever the circumstances, and whatever has been tried and failed, Chant-O-Matics will come through. Just follow the simple instructions given below.

FIVE CHANTS TO RETURN THAT WHICH WAS LOANED

These chants may be done on any day of the week.

Light your candles and incense (sandalwood recommended).

Sit for a moment and see the money owed held in *your* hand.

Sit, stand, or kneel and chant (any one of the following five):

1   Far, far, far away,
Moving off at speed.
Traveling with the speed of wind
To do the needed deed.
Near, near, near to me.
Returns that which was sent
Returns at once from whence it came,
To repay what was lent.
No bridges so short it will not reach
From me to friend in need.
No one way path that bridge of aiding;
Both may offer up their deed.
Whether proffering or repaying
Let the center-point be reached.
To connect the separate parties
And repay as it is preached.

2   Spinning round the Wheel of Fortune
Stops but where the Gods divined.
Sometimes mine, the luck of riches;
Oft times others do conned.
Let the wheel spin round about, then,
Let it turn to one in need.
But let that one be he who owes me;
Bring to him the golden seed.

3   In the mirror see reflected
Images, returned straightway.

All that's sent out is forthcoming,
Be it night or be it day.
Hold forth hands unto the mirror,
In return they're reached to you.
So that which I freely loaned out
Let it be returned too.

4 As tick, so tock;
And ding, so dong.
As one to other.
None goes wrong.
Rebound or echo,
Partner, mate;
Return to sender
'Fore too late!
As tick, so tock;
As ding, yet dong.
That which went out
Returns 'ere long!

5 To find the hole
Through winch one came;
To turn about; so back again.
Though there are problems finding ways,
The end result is "all repays."
Whatever reason for delay,
The route outlined will show the way.

Once committed let it rest,
For all will surely be for best.

Each of the above should be said three times in all.

FIVE CHANTS TO BRING MONEY TO ANOTHER

These chants may be done any day of the week.

Light candles and incense (sandalwood is recommended).

Sit, kneel, or stand and chant any of the following:

1 All have their needs that they try to will,
Sometimes the answer is not waiting there, still
Is it certain that with just the smallest of aid
No matter what debts, they can all be repaid.
The stronger my wish to bring fortune to others,
The sooner that blanket of good fits my brothers.
I know in my heart that all of my power
Will enable this needy one's fortune to flower.
And so I concentrate hard on this case,
The fortune wheel turns, and stops at his place.

2 It is not I who am in need
But one who's close and true.
To bring to him that fortune-seed
Is my desire to do.

That he may gather all that's gain
And use it wisely now,
To repay debts and ease his pain
Is what I would allow.

3 Not to me,
Not to me,
Not to me,
But to him,
To him, to him.
Money, money, money.
To him, money.
To him, money.
Not to me, but to him,
Money!

4 If a point of attraction is needed,
Let me be it.
If he cannot act for himself,
Let me act.
Yet do not direct the goodwill to me,
But to him.
Let me be the catalyst.
Let him be the recipient.

5 Mia libennay omtun forn-yeh
Clarius al perragus.

Ducellus, ducellus,
Decibum, decibum;
Fortuna, fortunis, elta inborris.

(Possibly bastardized form of early Latin chant)

How Chant-O-Matics Won Back for Tony E. What the Courts Could Not

▶   Tony E. is an author. He had written two or three quite successful books for one publisher when he was approached and asked to write a book for another publisher. Since he was not under any exclusive contract, Tony was happy to comply.

The book eventually came out and sold very well. Tony happily waited for his royalties—the percentage paid the author on income received from the sale of the book. But then one excuse after another was given to Tony by the publisher to explain why he had not received the monies due him. Once it was claimed that delay was due to a change-over to computer-held records. Then the publisher claimed that the computers were malfunctioning, causing further delays. One excuse after another was given. Tony's book continued to sell well, but Tony saw not a penny in royalties! Finally, there seemed no other recourse but to take the publisher to court.

The court experience was a frustrating, and expensive, one. Complications were set up because Tony lived in a different state from where the publishing company was located. Time dragged by and no headway was made.

Suddenly Tony remembered Chant-O-Matics. Some years before he had been to a study-group I had led, and had learned the principles of the subject, though up until now, he had not troubled to try the practical side. Digging back through his old notebooks, Tony found what he was looking for: the chant to return that which was loaned. He felt it fitted his particular case since he had, by writing a best-selling book, in effect "loaned" to the publishing company, who were due to "pay back" in the form of the accrued royalties.

Tony performed the chant and sat back to await results. He had not long to wait. By first mail the following morning, he received a check for the amount owed, together with a formal letter of apology from the president of the company.

How Chant-O-Matics Bailed Billy K. Out of Jail!

► Billy K. was desperately in need of money. He had, more than a year before, loaned $200 to a friend. The friend had never been able to repay the loan, yet now Billy really needed it. Guilty of a number of driving offenses, Billy faced jail if he could not pay the fines imposed on him. If only his friend, Henry, could repay the money owed, he would be all right. Yet Henry was penniless!

Billy was explaining his problem to the Clerk of the Court when the Clerk told him about Chant-O-Matics. "You'd be surprised how many people have bailed themselves out through chanting!" he said with a smile. "T know it sounds—well—unconventional, but give it a try. What have you got to lose?"

Billy did give it a try. He tried the chant "to bring money to another." The next morning he was awakened by a loud knocking on the door. When he opened it, he was faced by excited Henry waving a fistful of dollar bills.

"Guess what, Billy," he shouted excitedly. "I finally sold that old collection of postage stamps I got from my uncle. Turns out they were worth far more than I ever imagined! Here's that two hundred I owe you. Thanks a lot!"

6

A CHANT, NOT A CHART, WILL LEAD YOU TO TREASURE!

Many magazines and newspapers these days carry advertisements for metal detectors. These are based on the armed forces' mine detectors, and they sell like the proverbial hot cakes! Why? Because, as the ads explain, they "can lead you to *buried treasure!* . . . Gold and Silver Coins; objects of precious metal that have lain hidden for years—perhaps for centuries!—can be found by YOU!" There is a treasure-hunter in all of us, and we are only too ready to grab our metal detector and dash off in all directions to become rich the easy way.

But is it really as simple as that? In actual fact the cheaper detectors can only pinpoint large pieces of metal very close to the surface. Even with an expensive, super-deluxe model, what are the chances that we will be waving it over the ground exactly at the spot where "precious metals . . . have lain hidden for years—perhaps for centuries!"? The chances, we must ruefully admit, are scant indeed.

SO MANY PEOPLE SEARCH, BUT *YOU* CAN FIND!

That treasure-hunter side of our personality remains unsatisfied. Yet it need not. Why not do your hunting the really easy way, yet still have the excitement of search and discovery? Through Chant-O-Matics you can ensure that your goal will be reached; then set out to follow the trail. Let all the others wave their metal detectors laboriously over the ground. Let them pace up and down, their eyes glued to their meters or their ears encased in their headphones. Let them search—you are the one who will find!

YOUR HOBBIES CAN BECOME YOUR SECURITY

There are far and away more "treasures" to be found than Spanish doubloons and pieces-of-eight. There are many treasures out in full view, simply *unrecognized* for what they are! Once in a while you will read of the discovery of an incredibly valuable painting by one of the Masters. For years it may have hung on someone's wall. Sold at a flea market or garage sale for a few dollars, it was later authenticated and sold at auction for many thousands of dollars. The same sort of thing happens with old books, rare stamps, maps, dolls, magazines, and pieces of furniture. All are "treasures" in the very real sense of the word.

If you have a particular hobby, how much nicer to find your treasure through that hobby than through miles of walking and metal-detector waving. Through Chant-O-Matics that can be assured.

The 15 chants which follow cover all possibilities. The first five are good for finding such articles as rare books, paintings, stamps, and magazines. The following five are for antiques such as furniture, lamps, and autos. The final ones are for those of you who still would like to find that long-lost pirates' treasure! Whether you search the sands waving a metal detector; take your aqualung to dive in the Caribbean; or simply sit at home and try to deduce from clues gathered, the chants will lead you to your goal.

FIVE CHANTS TO FIND A RARE BOOK (*or similar*)

These chants must be done on a Saturday.

Light your candles and incense (any pleasant-smelling incense).

Imagine yourself—actually *see* yourself—with the rare book, or whatever, in your possession.

Sit, stand, or kneel and chant:

1 Capitare in mane al padrone,
E la farai capitare
In mano al padrone,

E le farai entrare
Nel cervello che se di quel libro
Non si disfara la scomunica,
Le portera, cosi questo dell' libro,
Verra disfarsi e col tuo aluto,
Verra portato alla mia presenze,
E a poco me lo vendera,
Oppure se e' un manoscritto,
Invece di libro per via lo gettera,
E col tuo aluto verra in mia presenza,
E portro acquistarlo
Senza nessuna spesa;
E cosi per me
Sara grande fortuna!

2   Swing goes the pendulum 'round and around.
Where'er it stops
There's gold in the ground.
Yet need we not dig
For the treasure is near,
And just at a glance
We'll see it so dear.

3   "Thou canst not see the wood for trees"
The saying is so true.
For when you look for treasures old
You must close look anew.

You must peruse where you have been
So many times before,
For there is where you'll surely find
That sought-for book of yore.

4 To me, to me, to me!
Word, word, word.
Line, line, line, line, line,
Page, page, page, page, page, page, page,
Book, book, book, book, book, book, book,
Page, page, page, page, page, page, page,
Line, line, line, line, line,
Word, word, word,
To me, to me, to me!

5 I gather and I sort,
And I place now here, now there.
As I gather and I sort,
I see not what I bear.
For I gather and I sort.
And I would not even dare,
As I gather and sort,
To find a book so rare.
Yet I gather and I sort,
And I know as I dig deep,
That my gathering and my sorting
Will bring me luck to keep.

FIVE CHANTS TO DISCOVER AN ANTIQUE

These chants may be done any day of the week.

Light your candles and incense (any pleasant-smelling incense).

Sit, stand, or kneel and chant:

1 No more problems,
No more strife,
No more troubles,
Or change so rife;
All will settle,
All will calm,
As the antique
I search for
Falls into my palm.

2 Just the touch of a hand
Stills the swing of the pendulum;
Just the touch of the gods
Stills the problems of life.
As the pattern of search
Turns one way then others.
So let now this chant
Settle all that it covers.

3 From the high seas
where the storms do so toss,
The ship noses into

The harbor, no loss
Is sustained to the crew
Or the cargo, for them
The waves are settled.
The storm would not dare
To ruffle the waters
Or upset the ship,
So calmness and quiet
Settle down into bliss.
A home found at last
No more wandering ever;
That chance that's so rare
Brings us two together.

4   All the time
Beneath the dust
Lying still
Beneath the rust,
Ever waiting, waiting, waiting,
Suddenly I'm here!

(*Say five times in all.*)

5   Brenigan, branigan, bronigan;
Brenigan, branigan, bronigan;
Chandler, chandler, chandler;
Hoy, hoy, hoy, hoy, hoy!

(*Say seven times in all.*)

FIVE CHANTS TO LOCATE TREASURE

These chants may be said any day of the week.
Light your candles and any pleasant-smelling incense.
Sit, stand, or kneel and chant:

1 Slow down the rhythm to a good steady beat;
Measure the paces to move marching feet.
Erratic no longer; no more moving on.
The location of treasure is now to be done.

2 Let the motion of the water,
As it swirls about a pail,
Gently settle from its moving
'Til it's calm and cannot fail
To soothe and smooth and lie so still,
To never more swirl round;
As I do settle steadily
And pinpoint what I've found.

3 Long will I lie in the warmth of the sun.
Long will I feel that my life has begun.
Long now and steadily, smoothly and true,
To treasure that's hid I'll travel straight to.

(*Say five times in all.*)

4 Yinkata, Yankata,
Yinkata, Yankata,

Yinkata, Yankata, Yinkata, Yankata.
Yeh! Yeh! Yeh! Yeh!
YAAARH _____! *(long and drawn out)*

(Say seven times in all.)

5 Bring me to treasure!
Bring me to treasure!
Bring me to treasure!
Steady, steady, steady, steady.
Let my future be soon ready
Steady, steady, steady, steady.
Let my future life be steady.
Bring me to the 'lusive treasure.

How Tommy W. Discovered a First-Edition Book Worth $100 in a 50¢ Rack

▶ Tommy W. spent most of his summer weekends traveling around New England looking through antique shops. He was especially interested in old books. He found that most of the antique stores invariably had a dusty set of shelves—usually at the back of the shop—with assorted volumes piled in various attitudes: Modern volumes of digested best-sellers rubbed shoulders with nineteenth-century hymnals and incomplete sets of the *Encyclopedia Americana*. Once in a while he would find an interesting old volume, perhaps dealing with shoeing horses or someone's travels in Outer Mongolia.

Always he looked for that hard-to-find item, a first edition of some well-known work. He had found first editions on a few occasions, but invariably of some little-known book worth no more than the fifty-cent price penciled on its flyleaf.

One day Tommy was going through the books scattered around an old barn. The owner was having a "barn sale" and along with the books were old 78 rpm phonograph records, rusty hand tools, glass bottles and insulators, and various-sized pieces of furniture. In the middle of a pile of five-year-old *National Geographics* Tommy came across a pamphlet on Chant-O-Matics. Intrigued he sat down in a convenient rocking-chair and started reading. By the time he finished he had earned a few strange looks from other browsers but was enthusiastic about trying the chants. He bought the book and took it home.

The following weekend Tommy carefully did the chant "to find a rare book" before setting out on his search. The very first place he came to had a lot of books and he set to work going through them. Expertly his eyes flickered across the titles. Suddenly his hand shot out. He had spotted a copy of *The Pansophy of Rudolph the Magus.* Ever the optimist he opened it up and examined it. "Published by Land, Sachs, Ltd., London, 1835" and, on the back of the title page: "First Edition, 1835." Excitedly he looked up and read the sign: <u>All Books on this Shelf 50¢</u>. He looked back down at the book in his hand, and knew it to be worth at least $100!

How Robert B. Dug up an Ancient Artifact that He Sold to a Collector for $500

▶ Collecting and trading old bottles was Robert B.'s hobby. He would take his spade and visit any one of a number of sites he had discovered and dig for bottles, which he later sold to a collector. There were several sites he frequented. They were all originally rubbish dumps, some of them so used for well over a hundred years. Digging carefully, Robert had found many rare bottles, most of them in good condition.

One day Robert's sister—one of my students—knowing of his hobby, read him some of her notes on Chant-O-Matics. Eagerly, before his next expedition, he did the chant "to locate treasure." He felt somewhat disappointed when, in his digging, all he unearthed was one broken bottle and an odd-shaped piece of stone. His disappointment changed to elation, however, when he showed his find to the collector who usually bought from him. The strange piece of stone, he learned, was a rare American Indian stone mortar, used for grinding foodstuffs, worth at least $300!

How Tracy B. Discovered Treasure While Still in the Middle of Her Chant!

▶ Sixteen-year-old Tracy B. was a great treasure-hunting enthusiast. She loved to read stories of the pirates of old and their buried treasure. She saved up her allowance and bought an ex-army metal detector, and would spend her weekends walking up and down the beaches of Florida, where she lived, hoping to find treasure. She even took to the water, in a rubber suit and flippers, in the hopes of locating a sunken galleon!

Tracy's desire for sudden wealth was not avaricious. Her mother was very sick and her father could not afford the necessary expensive medical treatments needed to make her comfortable, hence Tracy's at times desperate search for wealth. While other teenagers were enjoying themselves, Tracy never stopped searching. All her spare time was occupied in seeking out lost money or items of jewelry along the sands of the beaches. She was surprisingly successful, obtaining more perhaps than she would have gotten working on any job available to her. But it still was not enough for the very expensive treatment her mother needed.

Diana, one of Tracy's friends, owned a boat and one weekend she took Tracy out for a ride. They anchored offshore and Tracy, as usual, started diving. Diana sat in the boat and read through her notes on Chant-O-Matics, a course she was taking. On one of Tracy's brief returns to the surface, Diana told her a little of the power of the chant. She then searched out, and told Tracy, the chant to locate treasure. Tracy was enthralled. Repeating the chant to herself, she again dove beneath the surface. As she skimmed the bottom, chanting to herself, her eye caught the unusual outline of something half buried. Excitedly she started digging away at the mud and barnacles. What she eventually unearthed was an ancient cannon. Later excavation revealed the scattered remains of a sixteenth-century treasure galleon!

Tracy's find led to her mother's receiving the treatment she so badly needed.

PART THREE

Chant-O-Matics
POWER

7

CHANTS TO CAPTURE
THE HEARTS OF THOSE
YOU DESIRE

*I*t is said that there is no pain compared to the pain of loneliness. To need love; to seek love; to yearn for love, is to suffer soul-rending pain that is indescribable. Worse yet is to find love—yet find that it is not returned; to fall madly in love with one who either "doesn't know you exist," or who knows full well you are there, but is unable to find within that same spark that burns so brightly within you.

YOU CAN ATTRACT ANOTHER

In olden times many people turned to the local "Wise Woman," or Witch, seeking a love potion or something similar, to assuage this pain. High prices were paid for simple herbs or complex mixtures that were *guaranteed* to win for you the love of the one you desired. Unfortunately, these "guarantees" were frequently no more than wishful thinking—though the prescriber was never at a loss to explain why the potion failed!

Today no magical potions are necessary. Chant-O-Matics fills the prescription. And with Chant-O-Matics there are very real guarantees. If you wish to attract another, to gain his or her love, you have only to do one of the simple chants for that purpose, given below, and your desires will be fulfilled.

YOU CAN BEAT OUT ANY RIVALS!

It does not matter that you have a rival, or even a number of rivals, for the person's affections. Chant-O-Matics will see to it that YOU will be triumphant. No matter that a rival suitor seems to have more personality, more money, or better looks. These things are immaterial, for you will have more *power.*

YOU ARE A MAGNET
TO THE OPPOSITE SEX!

You will attract the one you desire as a powerful magnet attracts a bar of steel. All members of the opposite sex will take an added interest in you. They will go out of their way to talk to you, to touch you, to go out with you. The one who originally seemed not to notice you will now have his work cut out trying to keep you to himself.

As the power from a magnet may be directed in one particular direction, so will this power you acquire, through Chant-O-Matics, be capable of drawing from the direction in which it is pointed. Point it at the one you want, and he or she will be unable to resist, unable to turn back. He or she will come to you, perhaps without knowing why, but your attraction will be too great to resist. You will have won his or her love for as long as you wish to keep it.

A chant "to gain admiration and respect" will just as surely bring you that admiration and respect from any at whom you direct the power. This particular magnetism can be immensely useful in all aspects of life, gaining you advancement in your job or in your personal and social life.

Instead of placing your faith in a concocted "love potion," place it in tried and tested Chant-O-Matics . . . you cannot fail.

FIVE CHANTS TO WIN THE LOVE OF THE ONE YOU DESIRE

[*Note:* The chants in this, and succeeding, sections of the book, are of the *Mantric* variety. A *Mantra* (Sanskrit word) is essentially a *sound.* The sound has certain vibrations that generate "power." The ancients believed that miracles could be performed with *mantras,* since they had the power to create, sustain, or destroy. Sometimes the *mantra* is a single word; sometimes it is made up of a number of words. There is not, necessarily, any translation for these words since, as stated, they are basically just sounds.

In the practice of Transcendental Meditation™ one meditates on such a *mantra.*]

These chants should be done on a Friday.

Light your candles and incense (suggested incense: a mixture of Saffron and Peppermint).

Think, for a moment, of the one you desire and see him/her as being actually in love with you. After a moment or two of this thought, clear your mind and, sitting, standing, or kneeling—whichever is comfortable—repeat to yourself one of the following. You may say it aloud or to yourself. Keep up this chanting for approximately ten minutes, allowing no other thoughts to enter your head.

1 Malana, malana, malana, malana, malana, ...

2 Com mana, com mo; com mana, com mo; com mana, com mo; com mana, com mo, ...

3 Remenay, remenay, remenay, remenay, remenay, ...

4 Bhava devata, Shiva, Shakti, Vidya, Kala;
   Bhava devata, Shiva, Shakti, Vidya, Kala;
   Bhava devata, Shiva, Shakti, Vidya, Kala;
   Bhava devata, Shiva, ...

5 Roating, roating, roating, roating, roating, ...

FIVE CHANTS TO GAIN ADMIRATION AND RESPECT

1 Gayoset, gayoset, gayoset, gayoset, gayoset ...

2 Miranpeck, miranpeck, miranpeck, miranpeck, miranpeck ...

3 Kepser nanno rimda neegah; kepser nanno rimda neegah; kepser nanno rimda neegah, ...

4 Megelemer, megelemer, megelemer, megelemer, megelemer, ...

5 Om bahl om; om bahl om; om bahl om; om bahl om, ...

How Mike J. Won for Himself the Girl All the Other Men Were After!

▶ Janet M. was beautiful. So beautiful, in fact, that she was regarded as the "ideal girl" by all her male contemporaries— and not a few of her elders! She won every beauty competition she ever entered and, while still in her "teens," was offered a very lucrative contract by a model agency. In the small town in the mid-West where she lived, Janet was the envy of all the girls and the dream of all the boys.

Young Mike J. was working his way through college by playing his clarinet at dances and concerts. At one of the dances where he was playing, he first saw Janet being crowned Queen after successfully winning yet another beauty competition. He instantly fell deeply in love with her, but he was just "one of the musicians" so far as Janet was concerned. She didn't even notice he was there.

About this time, Mike attended a lecture I gave at his college. After the lecture he cornered me and asked some very direct questions about the effectiveness of Chant-O-Matics. It was soon obvious what he was thinking. Could Chant-O-Matics bring him his heart's desire? Could Chant-O-Matics make Janet not only notice him, but also fall in love with him? The answer was not long in coming.

Armed with a copy of a chant I gave him ("To win the love of the one you desire"), Mike set up a corner of his bedroom as his Chant-O-Matic workshop and, with much feeling, performed the ritual. Imagine his surprise when, at another dance a few nights later, Janet walked across the dance floor directly toward him! She started out by requesting that he play a particular clarinet solo— *Stranger on the Shore*—for her, but, at evening's end, many envious eyes watched as he left the hall with Janet firmly on his arm.

How Marge C.'s Directed Love Chant Got a Boyfriend for Her Roommate

▶ Marge C. was a tremendously likable girl. With a terrific personality, good figure, and great sense of fun, she never lacked a boyfriend. Marge's roommate Ruth, however, was a different story. Shy, somewhat plain, and with a noticeable stutter, she never had a boyfriend and continuously apologized to Marge for "being in the way," though Marge just as continuously assured her she was not. The two girls got along very well, though it was obvious—and perhaps natural—that Ruth envied Marge's success with the opposite sex.

It was a wistful Ruth who pointed out to Marge a short article on Chant-O-Matics in a magazine.

"Wouldn't it be wonderful," she sighed, "if it really worked, and if it were possible to get . . . well . . . to get a—a boyfriend through it!"

She blushed, surprised at her own brashness in giving voice to her thoughts in that way.

Though Marge's reply was noncommittal she made a mental note to peruse the article and, if necessary, follow up on it. She was very fond of her roommate and would do anything to help her find happiness. As a result some few days later, when Ruth was out for the evening doing some late shopping, Marge seized the opportunity to do a chant on the girl's behalf. Less than an hour after completing the ritual, Ruth returned home . . . accompanied by a bespectacled young man she had literally bumped into in one of the stores, and who seemed completely enamored of her and her nervous ways!

How Elderly Henry W. Found a Companion for His Twilight Years by Chanting Over the Telephone!

▶ Elderly Henry W. had expected to eventually get over the pain of losing his wife of some 40 years. Everyone assured him that he would soon grow accustomed to living alone and fending for himself. But being retired, and with no children to keep an eye on him, and with neighbors wrapped up in their own problems, Henry found himself sinking deeper and deeper into the morass of loneliness and self-pity. He tried to interest himself in various hobbies. He cultivated a small garden. He read books and watched television, but it didn't ease the ache for companionship.

He wrote something of his feelings to his only living relative, cousin Alfred, who lived over five hundred miles away. He was surprised one day to get a telephone call from the cousin. Alfred had been studying Chant-O-Matics and heartily recommended that Henry try it to ease his loneliness. Over the phone he gave a chant, which Henry repeated after him. Even if it didn't work, Henry reasoned, it could do no harm. It was a chant for love. It was not that he wished to forget his late wife, but just that he craved affection for his twilight years.

The day after he did the ritual over the telephone, Henry went to the local library and was surprised to bump into a lady he had not seen for almost 20 years. They had grownup and gone to school together. He was interested to learn that she was now a widow and, he found, feeling as lonely as he felt. It took no time at all for them to start planning outings together, and a long string of mutually gratifying meetings quickly developed.

8

CHANTS TO DISPEL LOVE AND BREAK-UP UNDESIRABLE FRIENDSHIPS

*U*nrequited love is bad enough, yet it is perhaps doubly painful when the object of your affection not only does not return your feelings, but also is deeply in love with someone else. It seems that before you can start to win affection, you must cause a rift between the couple.

IT IS NEVER TOO LATE TO TRY!

No matter how long the love of your life has been romantically linked with someone else, it is never too late to try to win the right person if your heart is really set. Don't feel that all efforts will be futile. They will not, for through Chant-O-Matics, your heart throb can still become yours. No matter what the odds seem against you, it is still possible for you to emerge victorious.

YOU CAN DRAW BACK THE ONE YOU THOUGHT WAS LOST TO A RIVAL

Initially you might have vied with a rival for a particular individual and lost. Many times the inclination is then to give up and either go looking elsewhere, or drink to forget! These are poor alternatives. Why give up? Why consider the matter closed? Why write him or her out of your life? There is no need, for you can still draw him or her back to you through the power of the chant. You can still come out victorious over your rival and he or she will be the final loser.

A PHILANDERING PARTNER CAN BE BROUGHT HOME

In some marriages there is the problem of one of the partners philandering. The husband may be having an affair with his secretary. Or perhaps the wife is having a romance with the mailman! Either way, the other partner can help bring the marriage back together by getting rid of the third party. To break up the love affair of these two will certainly contribute to the errant's returning to the nuptial home. Of the 10 chants given in this chapter, any one would be suited to this situation, though it should be remembered that "to separate a couple" is not necessarily the same thing as "to dispel another's affections."

FIVE CHANTS TO DISPEL ANOTHER'S AFFECTIONS

These chants may be done on any day of the week. Light your candles and any pleasant-smelling incense. Sit, stand, or kneel and chant (any of the following):

1 Mana rigo, mana rigo, mana rigo, mana rigo, mana rigo, ...

2 Val - - - - (*long, drawn out*) - - - - -, bola! Bola! Val - - - - -, bola! Bola! Val - - - - -, bola!! Bola! Val - - - - -, bola! Bola! ...

3 Sartot swer*tom*, sartot swer*tom*, sartot swer*tom*, sartot swer*tom*, sartot swer*tom*, ...

4 Vendurah, vendurah, vendurah, vendurah, ...

5 Aga, aga, aga; betol, betol, betol; markoo, markoo, markoo; aga, aga, aga; betol, betol, betol; markoo, markoo, markoo; aga, aga, aga; betol, betol, ...

FIVE CHANTS TO SEPARATE A COUPLE

These chants may be done on any day of the week. Light your candles and any incense. Sit, stand, or kneel and chant (any of the following):

1 Quadro, quedro; quadro, quedro; quadro, quedro; quadro, quedro; quadro, quedro; ...

2 Talinak melinak solinak voo, talinak melinak solinak voo, talinak melinak solinak voo, talinak melinak solinak voo, ...

3 Divide, divide, divide the two; each one, each one, each one anew. Divide, divide, divide the two; each one, each one, each one anew. Divide, divide, divide the two; each one, each one, each one anew ... ...

4 Swettle mettle voo ragom, swettle mettle voo ragom, swettle mettle voo ragom, swettle mettle voo ragom, swettle mettle voo ragom, ...

5 Nar, nar, noo, noo; nar, nar, noo, noo; nar, nar, noo, noo; nar, nar, noo, noo; nar, nar, noo, noo; ...

How Elizabeth W. Put Chant-O-Matics to Work to Prevent Her Long-time "Friend" from Stealing Her Husband

▶ Elizabeth W. welcomed her neighbor Betty into her home. Betty was a recent divorcee and Elizabeth felt it would help her neighbor get through the trial of separation to have her join in the activities of her family. Frank, Elizabeth's husband, didn't seem to mind Betty being included in their outings or even in their evenings home, watching television. In fact, at Elizabeth's request, he even drove Betty on various errands when her car developed problems.

Elizabeth and Betty became firm friends. It therefore came as something of a shock to Elizabeth when she found that Frank was doing a lot more for Betty than just chauffeuring her around! In fact, so close had the bond between her husband and her neighbor become, that there was every indication of another divorce fast approaching . . . her own and Frank's!

Sick with worry, Elizabeth turned to her sister for help. What could she do? How could she douse the flames she herself had fanned? Her sister calmly reassured her. There was no need to worry; Chant-O-Matics would take care of everything.

That same evening—while her husband ostensibly took Betty to do some shopping—Elizabeth performed a Chant-O-Matic ritual. She had not long finished it when Frank returned home, alone. He came to her, kissed her, and told her how much he loved her. She never did find out what had happened between Frank and Betty that evening but, for whatever reason, Betty never came to their home again!

How Mrs. M. Broke Up a Growing Affair Between Her Daughter and an Undesirable Boyfriend

▶ Mrs. M.'s daughter Susan had an unhappy knack of picking entirely the wrong type of boyfriend—from Mrs. M.'s point of view! A good student and obedient child, Susan started missing her homework assignments and staying out late at night with her latest beau, Harry. Rumor had it that Harry was heavily into drugs, and Mrs. M. naturally feared for her daughter's well-being. Susan constantly assured her mother that she was well able to take care of herself, but it was nonetheless disquieting for Mrs. M., and she would worry and wonder the whole time Susan was out on a date.

Despite Susan's protestations, the situation got worse rather than better. Susan's school work slipped badly and her teachers sent home notes about her change in attitude in class. Mrs. M. forbade Susan to see Harry again, but, for the first time in her life, Susan openly defied her mother.

Distraught, Mrs. M. consulted her minister. She was somewhat surprised when, instead of suggesting prayer, he advocated Chant-O-Matics! He had recently attended a seminar at which I had lectured and was very enthusiastic about its effectual use. He recommended the chant "to separate a couple."

Two days after Mrs. M. did the chant, Harry and his parents moved away out of the state and Susan—getting over the enforced separation surprisingly quickly—never saw him again.

How Chant Cooled the Ardor of Mary R.'s Unwanted Suitor

It wasn't that Mary R. did not want a boyfriend. It was just that she didn't want one right then. She was too involved with her nursing studies. There would be plenty of time for romance in a year or two, she reasoned.

But Mary was attractive and not unnaturally quite a few young men wanted to get involved with her. One in particular, named Bob, refused to take no for an answer. He waited for Mary when she left the hospital; he called her on the telephone every day; he wrote to her; he even followed her around the supermarket when she did her food-shopping! To Mary, Bob rapidly became a pest. It reached the point where she was afraid to leave her apartment for fear he would be waiting outside, no matter what the time of day or night.

Bemoaning her unwanted suitor to another nurse, Mary was introduced to the power of Chant-O-Matics. The other nurse had used chants for years to help in various situations though none, she admitted, quite like Mary's! Mary was willing to try anything. She took down all the instructions and hurried home to carry them out.

The next morning, as she left the apartment, she saw no sign of Bob. She didn't see him again for over a month. When she did he seemed quite indifferent to her—enthusing over his engagement to his new girlfriend.

9

THROUGH THE POWER OF CHANT YOU CAN BRING PRESSURE TO BEAR ON OTHERS

YOU CAN INFLUENCE OTHERS

It sometimes happens that you want people to do something and you *will*, with all your might, that they do it. When they subsequently follow your wishes, you are elated; but when nothing happens, you simply shrug your shoulders. Think how wonderful it would be if you could be sure of influencing them *every* time! With Chant-O-Matics you can. By doing one of the 15 simple chants given in this chapter, you can influence anyone to do virtually anything at any time.

YOU CAN DIRECT FORCES AT A GREAT DISTANCE

The distance you are from the person you wish to influence is not important. You could be halfway around the world from him or her yet still work as effectively as if you were in the next room! Distance is no object. The force-waves set up by Chant-O-Matics are powerful and are seemingly unaffected by distance, time, or even weather.

The action of Chant-O-Matics can be positive or negative. In other words, you can make someone *do* something, or you can *stop* him from doing it. If he is about to do something that would adversely affect you, then you can stop him from doing it. Yet if he is close to doing something you would like him to do but he hesitates, then you can give him that little push he needs.

SLANDER CAN BE STOPPED

A not uncommon problem is slander. Someone, for whatever reason, spreads rumors about you that are not true. There is seldom anything you can do about this, except run yourself ragged trying to counter the rumors. With Chant-O-Matics, however, you can relax at home and stop the slanderer dead in his tracks! It is almost as though you were *with* that person, "making the rounds" with him, as it were. And it's as though every time he opens his mouth to slander you, you are there to put your hand over his mouth!

NO NEED FOR YOU TO WAIT ON ANOTHER'S DECISIONS

How many times have you waited at home, perhaps for several days or even weeks at a time, longing to hear that someone has reached a decision on some matter affecting you? How many times have you paced the floor? Think how great it would be if all this worrying and waiting could be done away with. Think how wonderful it would be if you could decide when you wanted the decision to be made. No more waiting. No more worrying. With Chant-O-Matics you are the one in control. You are the one who decides when the decisions will be made.

FIVE CHANTS TO BRING PRESSURE TO BEAR ON ANOTHER

These chants may be done any day of the week.
Light candles and musk incense.
Sit, stand, or kneel and chant:

1 Quandro, quandro, quandro, quandro ...

2 Reab tab losa manna pin; Reab tab losa menna pin; Reab tab losa manna pin; ...

3 Chalaga, chalaga, chalaga, chalaga, ...

4 Doon venna leebo, doon venna leebo, dean venna leebo, ...

5 Quassi, quassi, quassi, quassi, ...

FIVE CHANTS TO BRING ABOUT A DECISION IN YOUR FAVOR

These chants should be done on a Friady.
Light candles and any sweet incense.
Sit, stand, or kneel and chant:

1 Revdo revdo rondi rond; revdo revdo rondi rond; revdo revdo, rondi, rond; ...

2 Swinit, swinit, swinit, swinit, ...

3 Turnaron, turnaron, turnaron, turnaron, ...

4 Brend brank, brend brank, brend brank, brend brank, ...

5 Toomit, toomit, toomit, toomit, toomit, ...

FIVE CHANTS TO REVERSE A DECISION

These chants may be done any day of the week.
Light candles and any sweet incense.
Sit, stand, or kneel and chant:

1   Twilstroo, twilstroo, twilstroo, twilstroo, ...

2   Backamon, backamon, backamon, backamon, ...

3   Vlendri domi quantus est; vlendri domi quantus est; vlendri domi quantus est; vlendri aomi quantus est; ...

4   Bregedar valtos; bregedar valtos; bregedar valtos; bregedar valtos; ...

5   Challolmer, challomer, challomer, challomer, ...

How Lennie C., Through Chant, Influenced a Committee to Accept His Proposal Though All Were Originally Against Him

▶ Lennie C. had invented a new system for use in firehouses. It was an automated system delineating the shortest route to a fire, with alternate routes shown and hydrant positions indicated. Although complex in construction, it was simple in operation, and promised to eradicate many of the prevalent headaches for the firefighters. Lennie was excited when after his demonstration of the prototype at his local firehouse, the fire chief and his crew enthusiastically congratulated him. The next step was for the city council to endorse its use in firehouses. The fire chief was not so enthusiastic about that possibility. He explained to Lennie that the council, to a member, was against any new expenses and was particularly wary of innovation. Lennie waited patiently, and hopefully, for a week then two more, but no word came. He had invested a lot of time and a great deal of money in his invention and was dependent upon its acceptance to pay many of his bills. Time went by and, although he asked what was holding up the decision, he received no satisfactory reply.

I had known Lennie for some years and, when he one day told me of his problem, I recommended he try Chant-O-Matics. I specifically recommended the chant "to bring about a decision in your favor." With a little more hope than he had entertained for some time, Lennie went home to do the ritual.

The very next morning Lennie got a call from the City Clerk. The committee had met the previous evening and had unanimously voted in favor of installing the new system in all firehouses!

How Fran H. Stopped the Slander that Threatened to Ruin Her Marriage

▶ Fran H. worked the late shift and, not having a car of her own, got a ride home each night with a co-worker. Fran was married but her co-worker, Bill, was not, and that was the cause of Fran's problem. Bill had quite a reputation as a "lady's man" and one or another of Fran's neighbors, seeing them drive up late each night, decided there was more to the situation than met the eye. Soon rumors ran hot and heavy around the neighborhood. The vicious tongues, having found such a situation, wagged harder than ever. It wasn't long before they reached the ears of Fran's husband, Ted. Ted loved his wife and trusted her, but he could not ignore the rumors and soon didn't know where he stood or what to believe. Fran was at her wits' end. Riding with Bill was her only way of getting home.

There was no one else with whom she could get a ride and she certainly could not afford to quit her job, which she eventually began to think was the only way to save her marriage. What was she to do?

Confiding in a friend, Fran learned, from her, of Chant-O-Matics. She determined to put them to the test. She decided to "bring pressure to bear on another." The "other" would be the scandalmonger.

Miraculously, it seemed to Fran, the talk suddenly died down, then finally stopped. People seemed to find new interests, new subjects for discussion. Her husband, Ted, forgot the vicious rumor and Fran retained her job . . . and her lift home every night!

How Mike W. Refused to Take "No" for An Answer

▶ Mike W. bought a parcel of land with the understanding that he could erect a building on it for the sale and service of campers and trailers. When he approached the town council for their approval on his proposal, however, he was told his plans had not been passed. Mike had given up a good job to go into business for himself and all his savings had gone into the purchase and projected enterprise. He had been led to believe the approval was only a formality, but now it looked as though he faced possible ruin. All his appeals to the council were turned down and Mike was in despair. It was his wife, Aileen, who suggested he try Chant-O-Matics. As she told him of their power, Mike regained some of his original spirit. He did the chant "to reverse a decision."

It transpired that the main reason for the negative decision had been the objection of one of Mike's neighbors. At the next council meeting, however, the neighbor, for no apparent reason, withdrew his objections and the approval for Mike's project was given.

How Pauline L. Got Rid of an Unwanted Tenant by Chanting Him Out of the House

▶ It wasn't that Harry J. did anything calling for termination of his lease. In many ways he was a model tenant. But Pauline L., his landlady, wished he would move out. She had first welcomed the security of having a man in the house. When she had converted the top floor into an apartment, she had hoped that just such a young man as Harry would move in. As time went by, however, Pauline found herself disliking her tenant. He seemed to have a sly way about him. She sensed that he was laughing at her, at her innocent preoccupation with television soap operas, her numerous cups of coffee throughout the day, her love for her cat, and the many other little bits and pieces that go to make up a lonely widow's world. She longed to have the house to herself again. Yet she felt she was not justified in turning him out without any valid reason.

Long a believer in Chant-O-Matics, Pauline L. finally decided to use them to rid herself of her unwelcome tenant. One night, after feeding the cat and having a final cup of coffee, she settled down to do the chant "to bring pressure to bear" on him. If Harry heard anything of his landlady's rite, taking place beneath him, he must surely have laughed it off as her talking to her cat!

But by the end of the week, Harry announced to Pauline L. that he had decided to move to another town. The job situation, he explained, was not all it had promised to be, and he felt obliged to seek fresh pastures. He apologized for leaving "just when they were getting to know one another so well!"

10

CHANTS TO HEAL AN UNHAPPY MARRIAGE AND BRING HARMONY TO THE HOME

"*T*ill death us do part" seems promise of many, many years of marital bliss. Unfortunately it does not always work out that way. The divorce courts are full of couples who feel that something other than death should part them!

MANY REASONS FOR AN UNHAPPY MARRIAGE

Not all marriages founder because of one of the partners being unfaithful, or miserly, or even cruel. There are many reasons for an unhappy marriage. Frequently it is simply incompatibility. Couples in the first bloom of love rush into marriage only to find out later that they really have nothing in common. That first bloom doesn't survive the first difference of opinion and there starts a gradual build-up of resentment, anger, frustration, and even hate. Some marriages, even today, are "arranged" by the couple's parents, for business or other reasons. These are seldom happy marriages.

Sometimes a couple is separated, in the early days of the marriage, by reason of the spouse's work. This is especially so when the spouse is in the armed services. When the couple does get back together again, they find that the original spark has gone out. Unhappiness with one another develops.

YOU ARE
THE MARRIAGE DOCTOR!

Whatever the reasons for unhappiness in the marriage, there are several ways of resolving the situation, rather than giving up and seeking divorce. Marriage counseling is one recommended path to follow. Let a "marriage doctor" diagnose and affect a cure. But then you yourself could be that marriage doctor! Yes, through Chant-O-Matics *you* could save the marriage and re-kindle that original spark.

YOUR MARRIAGE, OR ANOTHER'S

Of course it may not be your marriage that is at fault. You may know of a couple, perhaps close to you, who are having a hard time of it. You can see the unhappiness they are going through and long to help them and bring them back together again. Well, now you can. You can heal your marriage; or you can heal your neighbor's. Through Chant-O-Matics you have the power to do what even trained marriage counselors cannot always accomplish. You can heal an unhappy marriage and perhaps bring a couple together again, this time "till death do them part."

THE CHILDREN AND THE PARENTS

There are many marriages in which the husband and wife are extremely unhappy, yet they stay together "for the sake of the children." In actual fact they stand to do more harm to the children by raising them in an atmosphere of hate or near-hate.

How much better if harmony could be brought back to the family; if the unhappiness could be eradicated. Through Chant-O-Matics, this is possible. Through Chant-O-Matics, love can be brought back, between husband and wife and, subsequently, between parent and child. The 10 chants given in this chapter are, perhaps, the most important in this whole book.

FIVE CHANTS TO HEAL
AN UNHAPPY MARRIAGE

These chants should be done on a Friday.
Light candles and incense (Sandalwood, if possible).
Sit, stand, or kneel and chant:

1 Menda, menda, menda, menda, ...

2 Brento luna, brento la\una, brento luna, brento luna, ...

3 Meening, meening, meening, meening, meening, ...

4 Romana, romana, romana, romana, romana, ...

5 Sheel, sheel, sheel, sheel, sheel, ...

FIVE CHANTS TO REUNITE THOSE WHO HAVE SEPARATED

These chants should be done on a Friday.
Light candles and Sandalwood incense.
Sit, stand, or kneel and chant:

1 Manna, manna, manna, manna, manna, ...

2 Nilarta noseriff, nilarta noseriff, nilarta noseriff, nilarta noseriff, nilarta noseriff, ...

3 Shellem soovum quilten mo; shellem soovum quilten mo; shellem soovum quilten mo; ...

4 Lah, lah, lah, lah, ...

5 Shedow, shedow, shedow, shedow, ...

How Fran and Bill T. Recovered Their Lives Before It Was Too Late

▶ Generally speaking there is no reason why mixed marriages should not work. When they do not, it is often for reasons other than the obvious "crossing" that there is a break. Be it mixing of color, creed, social class, or even politics, there is no reason why two people truly in love should not make a goof it.

Fran and Bill T. were of different religions. They were young when they defied their parents and got married. Despite all the opposition, they felt their love for each other would conquer all. Perhaps it could have, but their "well-meaning" relatives would not leave them alone. Insidiously they worked on the couple till finally the marriage began to fall apart. Valiantly Fran and Bill tried to keep up a semblance of happiness. But each started to blame the other's relatives and, indirectly, each other, till there was little hope for the marriage's survival.

Linda, a close friend and earlier schoolmate of Fran's, watched what was happening in despair. She knew that Fran and Bill were right for one another and only needed a chance to get their marriage going without interference. She determined to help.

A Chant-O-Matic student of mine, Linda made Fran and Bill T.'s marriage her test case.

For greater effect she tied-in the chant "to heal an unhappy marriage" with the astrologically correct phase of the moon and really put her heart into doing the ritual. In no time at all, things took a decided turn for the better. Bill decided to take an early vacation from his job and took Fran away for a second honeymoon. On their return they changed apartments, refusing to let anyone—except Linda—know where they were, until they had really settled down. They made a pact never to listen to any gossip from any relatives and always to discuss any problems or doubts openly together. Linda claims you could see the love glowing and growing between them!

How Deidre C.'s Marriage-Saving Chant Changed Impending Disaster into a Second Honeymoon

▶ Alcohol was tearing Deidre C.'s marriage apart. Deidre's husband, Chris, was as close to being an alcoholic as it is possible to come. On paydays she knew she wouldn't see him till the early hours of the following morning, if then. When he did come home, his money was gone—drunk away. He did not care about his appearance or his job. He finally lost his job and, subsequently, drowned his sorrows in the local bars for two or three days at a time, drinking up his friends' sympathy. Deidre had been on the point of leaving Chris any number of times, but since they had two small children, a girl of two and a boy almost four, she felt she should not leave.

Knowing that Deidre was too proud to accept any offered help, her close friend, Sheila, subtly dropped hints for Deidre to take up Chant-O-Matics, suggesting that it would "take her mind off her domestic unhappiness." Of course Sheila saw to it that Deidre encountered the chants to heal an unhappy marriage. As Sheila had hoped, Deidre decided to do the chant.

Within 24 hours of Deidre doing the chant, Chris changed completely. He suddenly came home, showered, put on a suit, and only paused long enough to drink two or three cups of coffee before going out to look for a new job. From that day on he never touched another drink, though Deidre never did venture to ask him why he had changed so suddenly. She was just happy that he had.

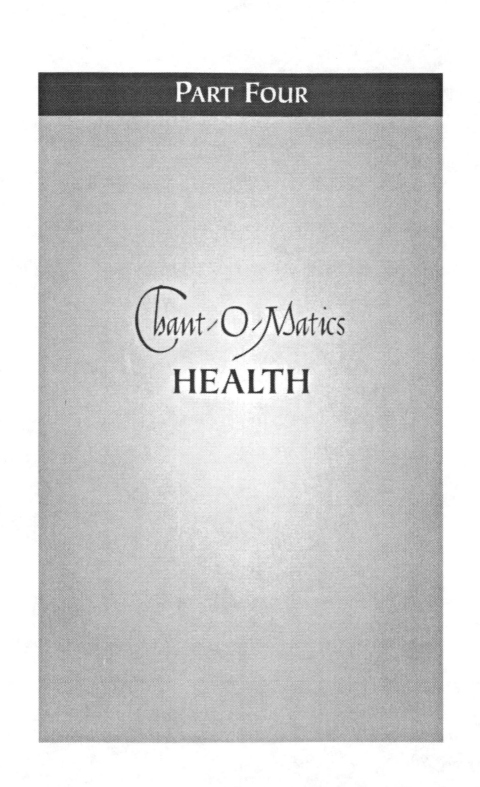

PART FOUR

Chant-O-Matics

HEALTH

11

YOUR HEALTH REGAINED UNBELIEVABLY, THROUGH CHANT

We are apt to take good health for granted. It is only when we fall sick that many of us realize we have neglected the all-important maintenance of our bodies. Then it requires extra special effort, and perhaps expense, to bring ourselves back to health.

THE MISERY OF SICKNESS

No matter how happy your life may be, no matter how much you enjoy your job, your marriage, your children, when you fall sick the world looks decidedly gray. There is no happiness in sickness. As you lie in bed, or huddled in a blanket with your feet up on the sofa, you know there are people out and about enjoying themselves. They are moving happily around living life, while you are suffering the misery of sickness.

There are few indeed who can retain their natural cheerfulness through the sniffling of a bad cold, the pain of stomachache, or the throb of a splitting headache. Yet think what a different outlook you would have if you knew that, no matter how sick you might be, you had the power within you to put yourself back on your feet and well along the road to complete recovery!

CHANT-O-MATICS CAN HELP YOU WHERE MEDICINE CANNOT

The common cold is one of the most aggravating afflictions you can suffer. You can cough and sniffle; you can gulp down aspirins, inhale vapors, take patent medicines, yet still it has to run its course. It seems that most people have come to accept the common cold as a nuisance that they must live with. They complain, but they go about their work or—at worst—stay home for a day or two to try to shake it.

Such afflictions, which don't seem to respond noticeably to medication, can be helped quite appreciably through Chant-O-Matics. To do any one of the five chants "to overcome a minor ailment" given in this chapter can help you immeasurably. Through them you will feel better, look better, and lose that depressed, miserable feeling of self-pity that so often accompanies the ailment.

RELEASE YOURSELF FROM DRUGS

At the opposite end of the scale from the irritations of the common cold, and similar ailments, may be found the "soul-possessors"—habituate drugs. The horrors of addiction to such drugs as cocaine, heroin, etc., are well-known to most, but what about addiction to such drugs as simple aspirin, diet pills, or even coffee? Many people are "hooked" on these without even realizing it.

Release from such drug habits is equally easy with Chant-O-Matics. To start down the road of recovery from such a serious illness (for drug addiction is indeed a serious illness), you have only to do one of the five simple chants given below for that purpose.

FIVE CHANTS FOR VITALITY

These chants (continuing to use the *mantra* form of chant) should be done on a Sunday.

Light candles and incense (Pine, Fire Apple, or similar is best).

Sit, stand, or kneel and chant, for approximately ten minutes:

1 Remma, remma, remma, remma, ...

2 Ergoo, ergoo, ergoo, ergoo, ...

3 Salaba Poten salaba vo; Salaba Poten salaba vo; Salaba Poten salaba vo; Salaba Poten salaba vo;
   ...

4 Akasa, akasa, akasa, akasa, ...

5 Tatum totum tatum vel; Tatum totum tatum vel; Tatum totum tatum vel; ...

FIVE CHANTS TO RECOVER FROM A SERIOUS ILLNESS

These chants should be done on a Sunday.
Light candles and any pleasant incense.
Sit, stand, or kneel and chant:

1 Necticoo, necticoo, necticoo, necticoo, ...

2 Regalsy (*soft "g"*), regalsy, regalsy, regalsy, ...

3 Preeva quilt, preeva quilt, preeva, quilt, preeva quilt, preeva quilt, ...

4 Sevren, sevren, sevren, sevren, ...

5 Sagosol, sagosol, sagosol, sagosol, ...

FIVE CHANTS TO OVERCOME A MINOR AILMENT

These chants may be done any day of the week.
Light candles and any pleasant incense.
Sit, stand, or kneel and chant:

1 Ethell, ethell, ethell, ethell, ethell, ...

2 Rezel mooning runner rite; rezel mooning runner rite; rezel mooning runner rite; ...

3 Warly, warly, warly, warly, ...

4 Mennen, mennen, mennen, mennen, ...

5 Seddler, seddler, seddler, seddler, ...

How Dorothy C. Saved Her Job by Cutting Down on Her Sick Days with a Vitality Chant

▶ Dorothy C. had a lot of minor ailments. She was one of those people who seem to be forever sick. If it wasn't a cold, it was a stomachache; if it wasn't a stomachache, it was a sore throat; if it wasn't a sore throat, it was an infection of some sort. Viruses many and varied sought out Dorothy so that she was forced to take days off work practically every week. She didn't enjoy being sick, as some few people do, it was just that she couldn't seem to stay healthy. Finally Dorothy's boss told her that if she took one more sick day she would be fired!

Poor Dorothy didn't know what to do. She could feel the symptoms of yet another cold creeping up on her. She took aspirins, cold tablets, syrups, and anything anyone recommended. It was no use. She could feel her temperature going up and up. She would go to work loaded down with tissues and inhalers and would sit sniffling and sneezing all day long, hoping and praying that she would make it through the week till she could collapse into bed for the weekend!

One morning, as she got into work all bundled up, she was told to report to the boss's office. "He can't be going to fire me," she thought. "I haven't missed a day—yet!"

But her boss didn't want to fire her. "Here," he said, "read this, I think it will help you and me!"

He gave her a copy of a booklet of mine on Chant-O-Matics. It included a section on **better health through chanting.**

"Take it home, read it, and try it," said Dorothy's boss. "I don't want to lose you, but I can't afford your sicknesses any more than you can. See if chanting can get you well."

The next day was Saturday and Dorothy spent most the day doing the vitality chant and speaking it over. She was determined to get well. By Monday she went in to work for the first time in months feeling wonderful. Her temperature had dropped to normal, her cheeks were their natural color, and she felt really great. Her boss was delighted to see her.

How Danny S. Astounded All by Healing Himself with a Chant, While the Doctors Stood by Helpless

▶ Although Danny S. was a student of Chant-O-Matics, it didn't at first dawn on him to try chanting for his own recovery when he suddenly fell ill. His mother rushed him to a doctor who, in turn, rushed him into a hospital. Danny had strange stomach pains that the doctors were unable to diagnose. Specialists were called in, tests were taken, meetings were held, but no one seemed to know what was the cause of the problem.

After a week or two of tests and x-rays, Danny began to get a little fed up with the fact that no headway was being made. Normally slow to complain, he now didn't hesitate to let his mother know how he felt. It was she who suddenly remembered Chant-O-Matics.

"Can't you get any sort of relief from your chanting?" she asked. "Of course!" cried Danny. "Why didn't I think of that before? Of course! Chant-O-Matics is the answer."

So, while the doctors still pondered the problem, Danny S. commenced his simple chant. He chose the one for vitality. Within 24 hours, Danny's mother was able to check her son out of the hospital. With the mysterious pains gone, and completely revitalized, Danny went on his way while the doctors still scratched their heads!

How Reesdon H. Amazed His Friends by Coming "Back from the Dead"

▶ Professor Reesdon H. was nearly 80 years old when he set off into the wilderness to do some excavating at an ancient archaeological site in South America. The institute for which the professor worked was not overly replete with funds for the expedition, so supplies were scant and personnel was at a minimum. There was a medical kit available, but no doctor went along.

The expedition was already overdue for its return when word finally filtered through to the Institute that the professor was stranded in the jungle with a bad case of malaria. Food supplies were almost exhausted and most of the native helpers had deserted. Many of the professor's old friends at the Institute sadly shook their heads. "This time poor old Reesdon won't come through," they said. "The odds are all against him."

But Reesdon was not so easily written off! In one of his brief periods of calm between the severe malarial attacks, he recalled his studies of Chant-O-Matics. Concentrating his remaining strength, he did the chant "to recover from a serious illness." The fever almost immediately started to abate. He felt his strength returning. It was an amazed "rescue party" that came upon the professor striding through the jungle toward them!

12

BAD HABITS ENDED THROUGH THE MAGIC POWER OF CHANT-O-MATICS

*A*lmost all of us have bad habits. Some are so slight as to be almost unnoticeable (the habit of saying "You know?" at the end of almost every sentence, for example). Other habits are much more obvious. The most common one is, perhaps, smoking. Where and how our bad habits got started is usually impossible to determine. But once with us they seem there to stay.

YOU ARE NOT A SLAVE TO YOUR HABITS

With things like smoking and overeating, it almost seems that you are a slave to the habit though this is not really so. You are only a slave for as long as you want to be one. If deep down inside you really want to kick the habit, then you can. You can draw on your power of Chant-O-Matics

123

to do this. There are 20 chants given in this chapter. By choosing one suitable for your particular problem, you can stop being a slave and become your own master once again.

YOU CAN OVERCOME ANYTHING, FROM NAIL-BITING TO CIGARETTE SMOKING

Nail biting, stuttering, overeating, cigarette smoking . . . all can be overcome through the power of Chant-O-Matics. For any bad habit you have, a cure is within your reach if you are willing to put your hands out and take it. Even if you have been smoking two or five packs of cigarettes a day for the past 20 years . . . you can stop! All it takes is (1) the true *desire* to quit, and (2) the Chant-O-Matics ritual. Apart from your health, think of the money you will save!

[*Note:* The words used in the next few series of chants are taken from old Gypsy magical cures. They should still be chanted in *mantra* style—i.e., the word or phrase repeated over and over again for approximately ten minutes.]

FIVE CHANTS TO STOP SMOKING

These chants may be done any day of the week.
Light candles and incense.
Sit, stand, or kneel and chant:

1 Shilalya prejia panori me tut; shilalya prejia panori me tut; shilalya prejia panori me tut; ... ...

2 Nani me tut kamav; nani me tut kamav; nani me tut kamav; ...

3 Anda kode prejia odoy; anda kode prejia odoy; anda kode prejia odoy; ...

4 Kusiden ferinen; kusiden ferinen; kusiden ferinen; ...

5 May kamen tut; may kamen tut; may kamen tut; ...

FIVE CHANTS TO OVERCOME A NERVOUS HABIT

These chants may be done any day of the week.
Light candles and incense.
Sit, stand, or kneel and chant:

1 Mashurdalo sastyar; mashurdalo sastyar; mashurdalo sastyar; mashurdalo sastyar; ...

2 Ava tu kiya mange; ava tu kiya mange; ava tu kiya mange; ...

3 Te kathehin; te kathehin; te kathehin; te kathehin; ...

4 Punra prejia, prejia prejia; Punra prejia, prejia prejia; Punra prejia, prejia prejia; ...

5 Trianda sapa the caven tut; trianda sapa the caven tut; trianda sapa the caven tut; ...

FIVE CHANTS TO GAIN SELF-CONFIDENCE

These chants may be done on a Saturday, Sunday, or Monday.
Light candles and incense.
Sit, stand, or kneel and chant:

1 De tre caveske; de tre caveske; de tre caveske; ...

2 Hin may tate; hin may tate; hin may tate; ...

3 Per de, per de prajtina; per de, per de prajtina; per de, per de prajtina; ...

4 Leskro sor kathe pashlyol; leskro sor kathe pashlyol; leskro sor kathe pashlyol; ...

5 Odoy ava kiya mange; odoy ava kiya mange; ...

FIVE CHANTS TO STOP OVEREATING

These chants may be done any day of the week.
Light candles and incense.
Sit, stand, or kneel and chant:

1 Sar e tcur avriural; sar e tcur avriural; ...

2 Sik lava, sik lava, sik lava, ...

3 Lava mange, lava mange, lava mange, ...

4 Andre pcuv tu jia; andre pcuv tu jia; andre pcuv tu jia; ...

5 Pcabuvel nashvalyipen; pcabuvel nashvalyipen; ...

How Geoff L. Stopped Stuttering and Got a Job as a Radio Announcer Through the Self-Confidence of a Chant!

▶ For as long as he could remember, Geoff L. had been the butt of his peers' jokes because of his pronounced stutter. He had learned to live with their wisecracks and even joined in their laughter when he got "hung-up" on a word or phrase. But deep down inside Geoff hated his stutter and envied others their speech. He would sit completely enraptured at public meetings and lectures, just listening to the flow of the speakers' voices, not even aware of what they were saying. In his dreams he would see himself as a velvet-tongued knight in shining armor, on a white charger, riding the countryside and charming all and sundry with his smooth eloquence!

Geoff was an avid reader. He would read anything he could get his hands on, for in his mind he could hear himself reading clearly and distinctly, without a sign of stutter.

In one of his periodic trips to the local library ,he picked up a copy of a book on Chant-O-Matics. It was in reading this that Geoff first saw the glimmer of hope that clarity of speech might not be forever lost to him after all. He decided to do the chant "to gain self-confidence," since he had long ago been told that lack of this was the basis for his affliction. As he did the ritual, he became vaguely aware that his voice was taking on a stronger, more confident timbre. By the end of the chant he was a new man.

Geoff's friends and acquaintances couldn't believe their ears when they heard that their "jester" had gotten a job as a radio newsreader. But every time they turned on their radios, there was the proof: Geoff L.'s strong, firm voice coming over the air without the trace of a stutter!

How Stan B. Stopped Smoking After 30 Years of the Habit

▶ It was obvious that Stan B. was a heavy smoker. His fingers were stained dark brown from nicotine, and his teeth were yellow. For over 30 years he had smoked cigarettes, working up to the point where he got through two packs a day. He couldn't really afford to buy so many, so he cut down on food and his health suffered as a consequence. He had developed an ominous smoker's cough and, since he didn't really enjoy smoking any more, excused himself by saying that he needed them "to settle his nerves." Truth was, he wouldn't have suffered from "nerves" if he hadn't smoked so much!

Stan wanted to give up smoking. He could see what he was doing to himself, but he just seemed to lack the necessary willpower to stop. He wanted to breathe easier; he wanted to save money; he wanted to rid himself of the stain and odor of the cigarettes. Then he learned of an acquaintance who had been in a similar situation and had quit overnight. The answer, he found, was in Chant-O-Matics.

So anxious was he to quit smoking, and so sure was he that he would be equally successful, that Stan flushed his remaining cigarettes down the toilet before even starting to follow the borrowed instructions! He had a few brief moments of uncertainty as he looked at the empty packet, but then braced himself and plunged into the ritual.

It was not until he went to bed later that night that Stan realized he had not smoked a single cigarette since doing the chant and, more important, *had not felt the need for one!* A smile on his face, he fell asleep happily assured that the 30-year habit had been broken.

How Kevin A. Finally Overcame Bed-Wetting and Its Embarrassment

▶ Most people associate bed-wetting with infants, yet there are many adults who suffer misery through persistence of this condition. Kevin A. was one such adult. It was his terrible secret. As a good-looking, athletic, young man, Kevin received many invitations to weekends away from home, but he had to decline all of them. He would have liked a roommate to share his city apartment, but felt it would be too embarrassing should such a roommate learn his secret. Much as he loved female companionship, he tortured himself with thoughts of sharing the marital bed!

It was the will of the gods, Kevin thought, when he read a resume of a Chant-O-Matic course I was to teach for adult education at a high school near him. He enrolled for the course and I could not have had a more attentive student.

With some slight hesitation Kevin approached me one evening and told me of his problem. Did I think Chant-O-Matics could help him? I assured him it could. Hopefully he planned to give it a try. Every class meeting from then on Kevin would come into the room and give me a big grin and a nod. All was well . . . week after week after week. The last I heard, Kevin was engaged to be married.

13

SOOTHE YOUR NERVES WITH CALMING CHANTS

*I*n this day and age it seems that many of us—especially city dwellers—live on our nerves. The rat race of existence; the scramble for transportation in the rush hours; the constant hubbub of noise; all these factors, and many more, contribute to near-shattered nerves and perhaps even the start of ulcers!

NO LONGER NEED YOU GET "UPTIGHT"

The expression "uptight" is very descriptive of this constant state of nervousness many of us live with. We feel a tenseness, a tightness. We feel our nerves are stretched to the absolute limit and, at any moment, may snap. Yet this being uptight is totally unnecessary. Even those living in the heart of a metropolitan area, in the very center of the "rat race," can live a calm, tranquil life with no fear of ulcers or nervous breakdowns. The answer, again, lies in Chant-O-Matics. That great power of the chant can be the very safety valve you have been looking for. Through the chant you can release the pressure and slacken that tightness till you once again return to your normal, calm, cheerful self.

YOU CAN RELAX WHEN ALL AROUND YOU ARE ON THE EDGE OF THEIR SEATS!

Apart from the build-up of tension brought on by your environment, there are occasions when even the most tranquil of us finds himself on the edge of his seat, as it were, with apprehension. This could be brought on suddenly by a near tragic or traumatic experience, or could be the culmination of a gradual build-up, such as the realization of your total indebtedness through unpaid bills! Either way you can find, and enjoy, the relaxation so important at that moment through Chant-O-Matics. Where others would be on that "edge of the seat," you can sit back and relax.

LIVE CALMLY WITH THE SOUNDS OF CIVILIZATION!

"Relaxation through Chant-O-Matics" might almost be the title of this chapter. It is certainly a phrase to remember. Relaxation is extremely important to all of us, but especially, of course, to the city dweller or the suburbanite who works in the big city.

Automobiles, jet planes, trains, jackhammers, pneumatic drills, motorcycles, power lawnmowers, chain saws, speed boats, go-carts, snowmobiles—the list of sound-producers in this modern civilization is endless! Every one of them is a contributing factor to your shattered nerves. Every one of them is another nail in the coffin lid of your nervous breakdown! Yet Chant-O-Matics can calm them all. Yes, the few simple chants given in this chapter can bring back your sanity and help you enjoy life again, calmly.

FIVE CHANTS TO CALM AND SOOTHE THE NERVES

These chants should be done on a Wednesday.
Light candles and incense,
Sit, stand, or kneel and chant:

1 Upro pcuv hin but pcuva: upro pcuv hin but pcuva; upro pcuv hin but pcuva; ...

2 Barvol barvol salciye; barvol barvol salciye; barvol barvol salciye; ...

3 Ada ada me kamav; ada ada me kamav; ada ada me kamav; ada ada me kamav; ...

4 Basa parro dsiuklo; basa parro dsiuklo; basa parro dsiuklo; ...

5   Predsia sirik leja; predsia sirik leja; predsia sirik leja; ...

FIVE CHANTS TO PREPARE YOU FOR AN UNSETTLING SITUATION

These chants should be done on a Thursday or Saturday.

Light candles and incense.

Sit, stand, or kneel and chant:

1   Pirano dsal mai sigo; pirano dsal mai sigo; pirano dsal mai sigo; ...

2   Avava adaleske; avava adaleske; avava adaleske; ...

3   Pechagerav momely; pechagerav momely; pechagerav momely; ...

4   When tute's a pirryin pre the drom; when tute's a pirryin pre the drom; when tute's pirryin pre the drom; ...

5   Ko chal robo avla; ko chal robo avla; ko chal rob avla; ko chal robo avla; ...

How Delia B., the Country Girl, Adapted to Life in the Busy City Through the Power of Chant

▶   Delia R. was born and raised in southern New England. Life, to her, was full of beauty. The only sounds she knew were the sounds she enjoyed—the sounds of Nature. It promised great contrast for Delia, therefore, when she made up her mind to accept her best friend Donna's invitation to leave their home town and to go and work in New York. Donna had long wished for the excitement of life in the big city and, though Delia was a little hesitant about the idea, she charmed her friend into going with her.

The two girls got a small apartment not far from the center of town, on the East Side. They were lucky in getting jobs as programmers in the same firm and everything seemed fine. But it wasn't long before the icing broke off Delia's cake. The novelty of riding the subway to work was fine for a while, but she quickly came to resent the pushing and shoving, the smells and sounds. She could never get used to crossing the streets and dodging the traffic. She began to long for the quiet and the peace and tranquillity she had left behind in New England.

She started to lose weight, and even Donna, caught up in the swirl of activity in city-living, noticed the dark rings beneath Delia's eyes and the brittleness of her nerves. She thought a new interest would help Delia and got her to enroll for evening classes at the University. Happily for her, Delia decided to take a course in Chant-O-Matics.

It did not take Delia long to realize that she needed help, and that Chant-O-Matics could give here that help. In a very short time she chose to do a chant for herself "to calm and soothe the nerves." She even talked Donna into helping her get things ready for it.

Within a week it was Donna who was trying to keep up with Delia! Donna was amazed that her roommate could be so active, yet remain so inwardly calm. She hadn't seen such serenity in Delia's face since they were lying out in the sun, beside the stream, back in their old home town.

How a Powerful Chant Let Mary Ann M. Calmly Run Her Eight-Children Home to the Amazement of Her Neighbors!

▶ Any mother can tell you that running a home, when there are two or three children in it, is a major job. Some mothers might even claim that to run a family with just *one* child in it is an undertaking! Imagine, then, trying to do all the chores, the shopping, the washing, the cooking, etc., etc., involved when there are *eight* children in the family! This was the case with Mary Ann M. Her youngest child, a boy, was 18 months old; her eldest girl was 14. Yet she was a model mother. Her children were always neatly dressed, and her home was in perfect order.

Mary Ann's neighbors were always amazed at what they saw. While they ran themselves ragged trying to cope with one, two, three, or perhaps even four children, there was their friend not only moving smoothly along, quite unruffled, but even giving of her time to such things as P.T.A. events! There had to be a secret to this sort of success, the neighbors decided, and over a number of coffee meetings, they elected one of their number to find out.

June T., the elected neighbor, had no trouble at all in getting the information. Mary Ann made no secret of the fact that she owed everything to Chant-O-Matics. She said she had tried other things, such as Transcendental Meditation™, but nothing gave such a fantastic return for such a small input as Chant-O-Matics. June T. made copious notes, and went running off to tell the others!

14

YOU CAN HEAL OTHERS THROUGH THE POWER OF CHANT-O-MATICS

*T*hat we all have healing power within us is demonstrated by the mother and child. When the child hurts himself, it only needs the mother to "kiss it better" and the pain is immediately abated, if not completely relieved. There is a certain psychological effect involved certainly, but that does not begin to explain even a small percentage of these innumerable healing incidents. No, the mother is able to heal through her *love,* and therefore her *strength of feeling,* for her child.

YOU CAN HELP YOUR LOVED ONES

This same form of healing can be used quite easily by *you.* Even without the mother/child closeness, you can still direct your healing energies, especially to loved ones. The mother, dealing with her injured child, has an immediate, automatic, connecting link formed for channeling this energy. You can form an equally effective connecting link through the use of chant.

YOU ARE SOMEONE TO TURN TO

Using the chant—and there are 25 healing chants given in this chapter!—you can develop your strength of feeling for the invalid to such a point that your relatives, friends, and acquaintances will immediately turn to you in their hour of need.

They will know that you are someone they can rely on; you will be recognized as their "natural" physician. And you will be a physician. By that I do not wish to imply that you should set yourself up in practice and adopt the title "doctor"! I don't think the AMA would be too pleased at that! However, you will certainly be on a par with any of the recognized spiritual and faith healers around the globe, many of whom have earned world-renowned reputations in this field.

EVEN YOUR PETS
CAN RELY ON YOU

Your healing powers are not restricted to your human friends. You will find that they work just as effectively on your animal friends also. A sick cat, an injured dog, a rescued bird—all will find solace in the healing powers you project through Chant-O-Matics.

FIVE CHANTS TO REDUCE A FEVER

These chants should be done on a Friday.
Light candles and incense.
Sit, stand, or kneel and chant:

1 Ima trava u okolo; ima trava u okolo; ima trava u okolo; ...

2 Korenja okolo jasenja; korenja okolo jasenja; ...

3 Vacarice coprenjice; vacarice coprenjice; ...

4 Un ramo forcuto; un ramo forcuto; un ramo forcuto; ...

5 A eto si udrijo vladiko; a eto si udrijo vlakiko; ...

FIVE CHANTS TO EASE SUFFERING

These chants should be done on a Friday.
Light candles and incense.
Sit, stand, or kneel and chant:

1 Ko u marcu; ko u marcu; ...

2 Wolosni wolosni wolosniceh um; wolosni wolosni wolosniceh um; ...

3 Te atuvici te rana; te atuvici te rana; ...

4 Urmen bactales yov; urmen bactales yov; urmen bactales yov; ...

5 Upro pirano ima ko; upro pirano ima ko; ...

[*Note:* The words used in the next few series of chants are taken from ancient Etruscan magic.]

FIVE CHANTS TO MEND A BROKEN LIMB

These chants may be done any day of the week.
Light candles and incense.
Sit, stand, or kneel and chant:

1 Folletto Tinia a ti ml raccomando; ...

2 Liberateci dalla saetta; ...

3 Sempre io mi raccomando; ...

4 In casa mia piu tu non possa entrare; ...

5 Testa in Tigna; ...

FIVE CHANTS TO REDUCE A NEED FOR NARCOTICS

These chants may be done any day of the week.
Light candles and incense.
Sit, stand, or kneel and chant:

1 Per mezzo di questa erba; ...

2 In pace sene vada; ...

3 Piu non avrai; ...

4 Teramo, teramo, teramo, che tu ai le simpatie; ...

5 Di farmi arrivare; ...

FIVE CHANTS TO BRING ABOUT FULL RECOVERY

These chants may be done any day of the week.
Light candles and incense.
Sit, stand, or kneel and chant:

1 Per il bene che ti ho voluto; ...

2 Sarei sempre il padrone; ...

3 A folletta di Norcia va ti a raccomodare; ...

4 Che la fortuna mi voglia ridare; ...

5 Mezzo di questa vada avrai; ...

How Margaret L.'s Life Was Saved by Her Sister's Chanting When the Doctors Had Given Up Hope!

▶ Day by day the doctors in the big city hospital watched Margaret L. sink lower and lower. She had been in a coma for almost 60 days from an overdose of drugs, and there seemed to be little that could be done for her. Margaret's sister and roommate, coming home late one evening, had discovered Margaret on the floor of their apartment and had guessed what had happened. Both girls had been heavily into the drug scene and death from overdosing wasn't unknown to them amongst their acquaintances. As with most dru -addicts, they felt that such an occurrence was the result of stupidity and couldn't possibly happen to them. But it happened to Margaret. At least, the OD part had happened and it looked as though death was not far behind.

One evening the sister, Janice, was sitting in the apartment smoking "pot" with several friends. The conversation, as always, centered around Margaret and her state of suspended animation. One of the group mentioned Chant-O-Matics, and the possibility that it might be used in cases like Margaret's.

"Why cases *like* Margaret's?" asked Janice, sobering. "Why not *on* Margaret?" As they discussed it more, they determined to give it a try. The following morning they got together again and, as a group, did the chant "to bring about full recovery." Hypocritically, they all smoked a "joint" before leaving for the hospital!

Janice was greeted by the hospital's senior surgeon. With a smile he informed her that, not an hour before her arrival, her sister had come out of her coma. Margaret was resting peacefully and all indications were that she had survived the crisis.

How Pauline S. Healed Her Dog When She Could Not Afford a Veterinarian

▶ Pauline S. bred Siberian Husky dogs. She didn't make much money at it, but it enabled her to keep up with her bills, so long as there were no emergencies.

It seemed the makings of a disaster for her, then, when she suddenly got a number of unexpected bills at the same time that one of her female dogs fell ill. They were bills that had to be paid—electricity, heating oil, etc.—and she knew from past experience that the veterinarian fees for a dog could soar out of sight! She obviously could not pay her bills and ignore her sick Husky. Yet, by the same token, if she had the Husky attended to, then the other bills could not be met.

The sick Husky was her favorite, as close to her as a human child. She *had* to take care of it no matter what. She tried various old "folk" remedies she had used successfully in the past on sick dogs, but it became obvious that the dog's illness was too serious for these. Large handfuls of fur came out of the dog's coat, and she lay listlessly in the corner of her pen from day's end to day's end.

Almost in despair, Pauline suddenly remembered some brief remarks I had made about Chant-O-Matics when she had met me a year before. They were to the effect that chant can do more for a sick loved one than any other medicine. Searching out my phone number, she called me and, almost in tears, explained the situation. I recommended the chant she should do, with full instructions on how to go about it. She thanked me and hung up the phone.

A week or so later, Pauline called me again. This time it was to tell me that her once-sick dog had just taken a ribbon in a local dog show. The Husky was in top condition and had never looked so good!

15

THE MAGIC OF THE CHANT WLL LET YOU RETAIN YOUR GOOD HEALTH

PREVENTION IS BETTER THAN CURE

Some of the old adages are incredibly trite, but one that is timeless in its truth, especially when applied to health, is "an ounce of prevention is worth a pound of cure." Why suffer unhappiness, discomfort, inconvenience, and all the rest of the trimmings of sickness when, by whatever means, you can prevent the sickness in the first place?

What are the best ways to prevent illness? Proper diet and exercise are the two most important, we are told. There is another very useful method, however, and that is through the use of Chant-O-Matics. Through Chant-O-Matics you can even prevent many of the minor afflictions, such as colds, sore throats, headaches, etc., that proper diet and exercise cannot always ward off.

NO ONE WILL BELIEVE YOUR AGE!

To many people one of the most ruthless of "afflictions" is that of old age! There are many, especially among the ladies, who would give almost anything to find a prevention for this! Yet there is a prevention, in a sense, through Chant-O-Matics. The power of the chant will certainly not *stop* old age, but it can and will eradicate all the signs of increased years. The wrinkles can disappear, the hairline stop receding, the paunch deflate, the double chin and the spare tire disappear, through regular use of one or more of the chants found below.

KEEPING IN SHAPE

Just as some spend 10 or 20 minutes a day working out in a gym, lifting weights or riding a belt-massager, so do others take but a few moments—perhaps only once a week—to repeat a chant. The chanters, I guarantee, look in better shape than the weight lifters. You can be one of these. You can amaze your friends by "stopping the clock," or even turning back the years. All that is necessary is to follow the few simple directions, which may turn out to be, for you, the elusive elixir of life.

FIVE CHANTS FOR BETTER LIVING

These chants may be done any day of the week.
Light candles and incense.
Sit, stand, or kneel and chant:

1 Tu che siei buono tanto; ...

2 Per quel giovane lo voglio fare; ...

3 Di Felicita e di buon cuore; ...

4 Sono a lume della luna; ...

5 In nome della tua bella; ...

FIVE CHANTS FOR CONTINUED VITALITY

These chants should be done on a Tuesday.
Light candles and incense.
Sit, stand, or kneel and chant:

1 In la sua buona grazia; ...

2 Questo e lo spirito; ...

3 Lo spirito Palo; ...

4 La buona fortuna ta lo farai; ...

5 Gran vino tu lo faral; ...

FIVE CHANTS FOR PHYSICAL FORM

These chants should be done on a Thursday.
Light candles and incense.
Sit, stand, or kneel and chant:

1 A vuoi mi raccornando; ...

2 Che siei tanto buono e gentile; ...

3 Pian piano sono un spirito; ...

4 Buona volenta; ...

5 Chiamami, chiamami, chiamami; ...

How Brian B. Astounded His Friends by Staying "Forever Young"

▶ Brian B. was a professional tennis player. He was accepted by his friends in the profession as a consistently good player, equal to if not better than most. He was fast on the court and was noted for the power of his drives, both fore- and backhand.

Practice is the keyword for all professionals, whatever their chosen sport. Brian B. practiced long hours, and was never the first to suggest calling it a day. Many of his fellow players indeed found it difficult at times to keep up with him, he was so energetic.

Consequently it came as something of a shock for most of them when one young player, casually going back through the record-books, noticed that Brian had been on the tennis scene for a good number of years.

"According to this," he told his astounded audience, "our 'young' Brian was bouncing the ball around the courts very capably nearly 30 years ago! That means, if he was 20 then, that he's now—wow!—he's nearly 50!"

It took a lot of nerve for one of the group, the following day, to bring up the subject to Brian himself.

"Sure," he grinned, "as a matter of fact I'm 49." He didn't look a day over 30. It was with great pleasure, and not a little humor, that Brian told his attentive audience how he owed it all to doing a simple chant for five minutes or so every morning, after rising.

"We thought you were the same age as us," said one attractive young lady. Brian winked. "Deep down inside," he said, "I am!"

How Jeanne C. Continued an Active Career for More Years Than She Dared Count

▶ As a professional ice-skater, Jeanne C. had to be in good physical condition, She was out on the ice every day, teaching figure-skating to her young students, telling them and showing them what to do. She loved her work and couldn't imagine the day when she would be too old, or out of shape, to continue. She watched her diet carefully and exercised religiously.

As the years went by, Jeanne found it harder and harder to stay in shape. Diet was no problem, but with her busy schedule it was becoming increasingly difficult to find the time to exercise as she should. She was frequently working in an advisory capacity for an ice variety show and so was not doing actual skating as much as she used to. Realizing that something had to be done before she got too out-of-shape, Jeanne decided to turn to Chant-O-Matics. She had used the chants successfully before, on many occasions, but never for this reason. As things were going, if she didn't do something positive in the immediate future, she would have to stick to advisory positions and never get back to her real love, the actual skating.

It was some months before Jeanne's work with the show ended and she put on her skates again. But the minute that she stepped on the ice, she silently thanked the power of the chant. She was in perfect shape and condition and, for as many years as she could see ahead, she knew she would continue her active career.

How Joe D. Did Ten Times the Work of Men Half His Age, Without Even Trying!

▶ Joe D. was a laborer, and much of his work involved lifting and carrying heavy weights, digging, and generally working under conditions that demanded he be one hundred-percent physically fit. His fellow workers were all young men no more than half his age. Joe would move around faster and more energetically than the best of them, never ceasing to amaze them. His boss was of the opinion that Joe did more than ten times the amount of work than any of the others did, and saw to it that Joe's paycheck reflected it!

Watching Joe D. work, his boss often wondered how he was able to keep up the pace he did. The boss could see the younger men wilting under the hot sun, dragging toward the end of the day, looking for excuses to sit and rest. But Joe kept up his rapid rate, almost running up and down ladders, swinging heavy boards as though they were nothing, working right up to the final whistle.

It was the boss, rather than one of his workmates, who finally asked Joe how he did it. He was astounded to hear that Joe attributed it all to the power of the chant. Long a student of Chant-O-Matics, Joe daily practiced the chant for continued vitality. His work, day after day, month after month, and year after year, attested to the success of his plan.

PART FIVE

Chant-O-Matics
PROTECTION

16

THE MIGHTY POWER OF CHANT TO PROTECT YOU FROM EVIL

YOUR ENEMIES, KNOWN AND UNKNOWN

There are few people indeed who can honestly say they do not have an enemy. Many people do not *deserve* to have an enemy, certainly, but that is not the same thing. Enemies can result from envy, jealousy, imagined wrongs, or even from illogical thinking. You may feel you do not have an enemy in the world, yet someone you consider a good friend may, in reality, be so indescribably jealous of your general popularity that he or she is sending you negative thoughts every minute of the day. And this is really the crux of the matter: Thought is tantamount to deed! If someone wishes you ill strongly enough, then you will receive that ill. This is the whole basis of Black Magic and so-called "Voodoo Dolls."* But through Chant-O-Matics

---

° See *A Pocket Guide to the Supernatural*, Buckland, Ace Books, New York, N.Y., 1975.

you can give yourself a Circle of Protection against even the most insidious attack.

THE FEAR OF POSSESSION

Not only is there danger of "attack" from this plane of being, but also from other planes. This point was brought home strongly by the book and the movie *The Exorcist*, in which a young girl was possessed by a malevolent spirit. Although the story was fiction, it was based on actual fact. There have been many cases of possession by evil spirits, though you must not jump to the conclusion that it is possession by "the Devil" (if there is such an entity!).

The impact of *The Exorcist* had both bad and good effects. It was bad in that it caused numerous instances of hysterical, or psychological, possession: i.e., people *believed* themselves to be possessed (though in actual fact they were not) and acted accordingly. It was good in that it did make people aware of the *possibility* of possession, and opened their eyes to a whole new world of the occult. Knowledge of the occult leads you to understand, and therefore to lose your fear (for fear is based on ignorance) of the supernormal.

As Chant-O-Matics can protect you from attack on this plane, so can it equally protect you from attack—even in the form of possession—from other planes. Had Regan MacNeil, the young girl in *The Exorcist*, or her mother known of the power of the chant, she would never have succumbed to her demonic usurper.

YOU CAN FIGHT
PSYCHIC VAMPIRES!

Each of us has an *aura*. This is an invisible emanation that comes from your body. It is visible to psychics—and even to the ordinary person under the right conditions*—and is the basis of the "halo" used by artists for centuries to depict radiant holiness.

There are many people who are what would be termed "Psychic Vampires." They may not know they are such, yet that does not negate their damaging influence on others. Have you ever been in the presence of someone who left you feeling absolutely exhausted? You may even have thought of yourself as being "drained." Well, drained you were, in no uncertain manner! What happened was that that person, a Psychic Vampire, drained your aura. A vampire of this type needs energy, and burns it up very quickly. To supplement his own inadequate supply, he attacks you (psychically and, nine times out of ten, without even being aware that he is doing so) and draws off your energy. This (1) depletes your aura and leaves you mentally and physically exhausted, and (2) removes your psychic protective shield, leaving you open to attack by any and every malevolent entity so inclined!

Once again, your sure means of defense is Chant-O-Matics. The power of the chant can give you more than adequate protection after such vampiric attack while you

---

* See *Amazing Secrets of the Psychic World*, Buckland and Carrington, Parker Publishing Co., Inc., West Nyack, N.Y., 1975.

rebuild your psychic energies. It can also give you—remembering, from Chapter 15, that prevention is better than cure—iron-clad protection from any such attack in the first place!

YOUR INCREDIBLE HIDDEN POWER

The power locked within you is truly amazing! It can be used in so many ways to read people's minds (E.S.P.); to move objects without physical contact (Psychokinesis); to diagnose and prescribe for sickness (medical radiesthesia); to see and hear the dead (clairvoyance and clairaudience); and many, many more exciting things. But surely the most exciting, and truly the most utilitarian, way to use this power is to protect yourself from all possible forms of evil. How to use it in this manner? Why, through the simple process of Chant-O-Matics.

[*Note:* The words used in the final series of chants are taken from ancient Anglo-Saxon magical charms. They should be chanted in *mantra* style.]

FIVE CHANTS FOR A CIRCLE OF PROTECTION

These chants may be done on any day of the week.
Light candies and incense.
Sit, stand, or kneel and chant:

1 God cweeth eak swilch; ...

2 Bare nu lairt on hear; ...

3 God gewort there airdan dior; ...

4 Ik eom driten hin; ...

5 Ne stel thu; ...

FIVE CHANTS AGAINST UNKNOWN ENTITIES

These chants may be done any day of the week.
Light candles and incense.
Sit, stand, or kneel and chant.

1 Ne synga thu; ...

2 No bare thu on leesra; ...

3 Ne his oxan ne; ...

4 Hig gesawon tha; ...

5 Maistan ofermettu genitherode; ...

FIVE CHANTS TO REINFORCE YOUR AURA

These chants should be done on a Saturday.
Light candles and incense.
Sit, stand, or kneel and chant:

1 Gewaird thaitter sunu; ...

2 Ful tien winter; ...

3 Tida and flu thissa; ...

4 Getimbred from twam; ...

5 Him from afaran het; ...

How Curtis F. Exorcised Himself of a Possessing Demon with an Irresistibly Powerful Chant

▶ The realization of possession was slow in coming to Curtis F. Perhaps he suspected the truth long before he dared admit it, to himself or to his friends, but he sought everywhere else for a believable explanation. There was none forthcoming. He found himself doing things that he not only did not want to do, and would never do under normal circumstances, but things that he fought with himself to avoid doing! He loved animals. He had eight pet rabbits, which he had reared from babies. They were beautiful Persian Blues, with delicately soft, silky, smoky-gray coats. He loved the rabbits and called them each by name! Yet one morning, for no apparent reason, he took them one by one, killed them, and skinned them for their pelts! Tears streamed down his face as he did it, but he could not stop himself! He had no control over his actions. It was as though he was an unwilling spectator trapped inside his own body.

Fear gripped him as he saw himself viewing next the beautiful coat of his beloved dog, a golden retriever. With a cry of terror Curtis forced himself to run from the house and keep running, till he finally fell exhausted at the side of the road.

Whatever was possessing him then, seemed to leave him free for a few days. In those few days, Curtis talked with all his closest friends, seeking and even pleading for help. One of them was finally able to offer a ray of hope.

It was Chant-O-Matics.

"I don't know if it's powerful enough for this," said the friend, a student of mine, "but I can sure find out. From what I've seen of its effects in the past, though, I'm sure you have nothing to worry about,"

He was right. I sent Curtis a chant "against unknown entities." From the day he did the ritual he had no further trouble. "Somehow," he said, "I feel as though I have been thoroughly cleansed. I feel great!"

How Rosalie W. Drove a Chant-O-Matic "Stake" Through the Heart of a Psychic Vampire!

▶ Rosalie W. was well read in the occult. Consequently it didn't take her long to realize what was happening when she found herself, repeatedly, exhausted on her return home from a weekly psychic-development group she attended. It was to be expected that she would feel a certain exhaustion from some of the exercises and experiments conducted at these meetings, but she knew she was feeling far more completely drained on far too many occasions for it to be natural. It did not take her long to find that the most probable cause was a Psychic Vampire in the group!

The next step for Rosalie was, of course, to find which of the ten people in the group was the vampire. Almost certainly that person did not know that he or she was such. By carefully questioning the individuals, Rosalie had no difficulty in narrowing down the suspect to Mildred M., a little old lady with, apparently, an excess of nervous energy. Rosalie now realized that it was *her* energy, and that of the others in the group, that Mildred was burning up so rapidly.

The next step was to seek a cure. Not just a protection for herself and the rest of the group, but also an end to Mildred's psychic attacks was what Rosalie wanted. She finally decided that the strongest and surest means to achieve these ends was to use the power of Chant-O-Matics. First of all, she reinforced everyone's aura, including Mildred's. Then she placed a Circle of Protection around Mildred M. If she had only protected those in the group *other than* Mildred it would have been enough—for the group. But she had to think of all the other people Mildred encountered in her everyday life. They had to be protected, too. So, by placing the protection around Mildred, she (1) conserved the old lady's energy by stopping-up the outlet/inlet "fangs" of the Psychic Vampire, and (2) protected Mildred from any damage she might do to herself in "attacking" a (psychically) evil person.

17

UNCROSS YOURSELF WITH CHANTS THAT CAN BREAK ALL CURSES!

Some people scoff at the very idea of curses—until they encounter one themselves! Curses are very real to a great many people. They should be treated with respect.

PEOPLE OF ALL KINDS HAVE BEEN CROSSED BY OTHERS

In the previous chapter I spoke of how you might inadvertently acquire enemies without any conscious effort on your own part. It is unfortunate, but happily rare, that some of these enemies find the way to effectively curse those they dislike. The curse may be no more than an extremely strong desire or wish on their part. I know of a case, for example, where a woman had been made supervisor of a factory shift and one of the other women resented the fact that *she* did not get the promotion. By whatever distorted reasoning she used, she decided to avenge this slight by cursing the new supervisor. She literally "wished" the woman into a nasty factory accident!

I know of another case where a man became personal secretary to a millionaire. Although the millionaire had taken the man, almost literally, "off the streets" and had given him a position of responsibility with an extremely fine salary, the man *resented* the fact that *he* had not been born a millionaire. Outwardly loyal and friendly to his employer, the man surreptitiously hired a Haitian *Boko* to place a fatal curse on him. The millionaire died in a fiery car crash and, though the secretary inherited several thousand dollars, he remained disgruntled that he had originally been born into a poor family!

YOU MAY HAVE BEEN CROSSED WITHOUT KNOWING IT!

The tragedy is that, as in the cases cited, it is possible to be crossed, or cursed, without knowing it until too late. If either of the two people above had known they had been crossed, they might well have spared themselves their accidents by taking preventive measures. It is well, periodically, to take stock of your situation in life, or even a particular aspect of your life such as your job. Try to see yourself from the points of view of those with whom you come into contact, and especially those who work closely with you. If you have any known enemies, study them closely. Try to think the way they would think.

Decide whether or not any of these friends and/or enemies are the type to cross you. Do any of them have a background of, or interest in, any aspects of the occult?

YOU CAN WALK UNAFRAID

There is no need for you to become paranoid over this. If there was no way you could protect yourself from possible crossing, then there might be some excuse for tendency to panic! But there is a very fine form of protection available to you . . . Chant-O-Matics.

You can walk unafraid when you know that a simple chant can spare you from whatever might be wished upon you by even your worst enemy. You can save yourself any sort of unpleasantness and, as easily, can save anyone else you know to be threatened. A mother can protect her child; a friend, his neighbor. Indeed it is often easier to see what is happening to another than it is to recognize what is happening to yourself. The 10 simple chants given in this chapter can free you, or another, from anything that might be directed.

FIVE CHANTS TO UNCROSS ANOTHER

These chants should be done on a Saturday.
Light candles and incense.
Sit, stand, or kneel and chant:

1 Betwy noradial and westdial; ...

2 Walstmum on treowum; ...

3 Swylca eek theos; ...

4 Forthgongenre tide; ...

5 Eardungstowe cynn nu; ...

FIVE CHANTS TO FREE YOURSELF

These chants may be done any day of the week.
Light candles and incense.
Sit, stand, or kneel and chant:

1 Camp sum sing niht; ...

2 Lufian fela; ...

3 Hal, lufian, hand; ...

4 Gemunde ic eak hu; ...

5 Swelka hi kwaiden; ...

How George B. Miraculously Broke the "Curse" He Had Suffered Under for So Long

▶ His aged mother insisted to George B. that an ex-suitor of hers had cursed her future son when she married George's father. George did not believe the story, or claimed he did not, but there was no denying the fact that nothing had gone right for him from the day he was born. He had been a "blue" baby; had suffered every imaginable childhood disease; did miserably in school; never kept a girlfriend more than a week; never kept a job more than a month; smashed his new car the first day he got it—the list was never-ending. It was not surprising, then, that when George eventually met a really wonderful girl—one he dearly wished to marry—he started desperately searching for a way to shake off the long-standing curse.

George felt he had a diamond in his grasp, but that he tottered on the brink of an abyss. He might drop the diamond, or he might fall over the edge, or perhaps even both. Never had he wanted anything so much. He was determined to hold on and step back to solid ground.

Having no other friends in whom to confide, George eventually told his story, and his fears, to his girlfriend. He was half afraid, with his record, that she would think him crazy and leave him right then and there.

Happily she did not. In fact, she was extremely sympathetic. She had heard of people being crossed before and she even had a possible solution for George—Chant-O-Matics.

George was elated. He was willing to try anything and eagerly prepared for the ritual to free himself. It didn't take long and, after he did it, he half expected there would be a clap of thunder or a flash of lightning, or something similar! There was nothing. Instead the days passed, and passed . . . and George and his girlfriend stayed together. He got a good lob; they married; things went extremely well and—as the old fairy tales would have it—they lived happily ever after!

How Amy C. Changed from "Calamity Jane" to "Lucky Lucy" with a Single Chant

▶ "Calamity Jane" was the only name that truly fitted Amy C. It seemed that everything she touched turned to dust. It wasn't just that she was clumsy, though that she certainly was! Anything with which she became involved would disintegrate. One winter the local church group was raffling a new car to raise money for charity. Amy joined the committee and set out to sell tickets. Her jalopy skidded on a patch of ice and she careened across the high street, through a plateglass window, and smashed into the side of the prize automobile sitting on display. She took the Girl Scouts on a camping trip, and it rained, with thunderstorms, for ten days!

She had a barbeque, moved the burners into the garage when it started raining, and started a fire that burned down the garage! She was bridesmaid at her sister's wedding, stepped on the hem of the bride's gown, and left the bride standing half-naked in the church aisle!

There seemed no good reason for Amy's many calamities. Boyfriends fled from her. Many people said she was cursed, but there was no real evidence for that as a fact. She needed uncrossing.

It was her sister, Jane, the hapless bride she had "defrocked," who offered the solution.

"Try Chant-O-Matics," said Jane. "I've used them for years, and owe my home and happiness to the power of chant. Here, let me write down what you have to do."

It was a simple chant and even Amy couldn't do it wrong. As soon as she had finished it, she felt strangely elated. A warm, comforting calm seemed to spread over her body.

Calmly she sat back to soak up a confidence in herself she had never known before.

Things changed at a rapid, head-spinning pace for Amy. Suddenly everything she touched turned to gold. She could do nothing wrong. It was her sister who nicknamed her "Lucky Lucy." Soon it was "Lucky Lucy" who was walking down the wedding aisle.

18

PURIFICATION THROUGH CHANT

THE "SENSE OF EVIL" IN A HOUSE OR A PERSON

It is not uncommon to go into a house, or one particular room in a house, and feel an all-pervading sense of evil that causes shivers to run up and down your spine. It is less common, but by no means unknown, to meet a person who has this same effect on you. The reasons may be many. With a house it is invariably the result of some traumatic event that took place there, perhaps many years before. With a person it could be a case of possession (dealt with in Chapter 16), or it could be an actual evil that permeates that person's very soul. This may be the result of a bad early childhood, of a series of misfortunes, circumstances, bad choice of friends, or any one of a dozen reasons. Happily there are few people of this caliber in everyday life, but don't completely rule out the possibility of running into one.

YOUR CONFIDENCE AND ABILITY CAN HELP OTHERS

Where do you go for help when you own such an evil house, or have someone near and dear to you who seems to bear the stamp of evil? These are not uncommon problems, yet the average person is completely floored when confronted with such a situation. There is certainly no service listed in the Yellow Pages to cover the problems! No, it is only through word of mouth that you can find a person who has the knowledge and the ability to purify the inherent evil. Such people are much sought after for the confidence and assurance they can give the one with the problem. They earn, and deserve, great respect.

YOU could be that person! You could be the one to whom they turn in their hour of need. You could have the confidence and the ability to help others.

YOU, THE EXORCIST!

With a knowledge of Chant-O-Matics you have the power to purify, be it house, person, object, or whatever. You are, through the power of chant, the most effective Exorcist there is. For, as has been seen in the preceding chapters, chant is the funnel through which you can direct those powerful forces that lie dormant within all of us, waiting to be awakened and called upon for service. What better direction to send those forces than to the purification of an invaded person or thing?

FIVE CHANTS TO PURIFY A HOUSE OR BUILDING

These chants should be done on a Saturday.
Light candles and incense.
Sit, stand, or kneel and chant:

1 Ond eft sway same geliornodon; ...

2 Eallum monnum to wiotonne; ...

2 Airestan skipu manna Angel; ...

4 There wearch micel wale; ...

5 Gefeaht gefliemde; ...

FIVE CHANTS TO PURIFY AN OBJECT

These chants should be done on a Saturday.
Light candles and incense.
Sit, stand, or kneel and chant:

1 Bestailon there fierde; ...

2 Escanseaster ong; ...

3 Gegaderade cyming; ...

4 Mistra daga eelchy othe his fierde; ...

5 Airest skeop airone bearn; ...

FIVE CHANTS TO PURIFY A PERSON

These chants may be done any day of the week.
Light candles and incense.
Sit, stand, or kneel and chant:

1 Tela, wuton we wel thair; ...

2 Gesegnode wuton bolstra tha; ...

3 Eelum incan blide to him; ...

4 Ond mid thy he bair; ...

5 Dyde hwair swa kewed; ...

How Larry M. Bought a "Haunted" House Cheaply, Purified It Through Chant, and Then Sold It at a $27,090 Profit!

▶ Larry M. and his wife, Eunice, looked over the house with growing excitement. Married almost three years, and with a baby on the way, they dearly wished to get out of their apartment and own their own house. But with the skyrocketing price of real estate, together with the smallness of the nest egg they had been able to put away toward the down payment, it seemed impossible that their dream could come true. It was with more hope than they dared show that they had gone to view the old Victorian house advertised at the ridiculously low price of $58,000. Small by Victorian standards, yet large compared to modern homes, the house obviously needed the work of a handy-man to bring it back into shape. Larry didn't mind that. If it became *their* house, as they both hardly dared hope it would, he would repair it and paint it with loving care. He could make it a show-place, he knew.

"Well?" asked the real-estate salesman. "What do you think? Are you interested?" He seemed somewhat nervous, and anxious to get it over with.

"Of course we're interested," said Larry. Eunice's squeeze of his hand told him how she felt about it.

It wasn't till some weeks later, when the deal had been made and they had moved in, that they found the reason for the Realtor's nervousness. From a neighbor they found-out, indirectly, that their house was haunted!

"So that's why it was so cheap," said Eunice, with a shiver. "I guess they couldn't get anyone else to buy it!"

Larry was not dismayed. He had long suspected the truth, though had not discussed it for fear of upsetting Eunice. Apparently, however, she too had had her suspicions and now she voiced them. They both agreed that it was the spare bedroom—projected nursery—that was the seat of the evil emanations. Later investigation showed that it was indeed in that room, many years before, that a brutal murder had taken place.

Eunice became upset. Her personality gradually changed. She lost her normal vivacity and became withdrawn and broody. Larry sensed that she was beginning to dread the time when they would bring the baby into the house. Something had to be done, and done quickly.

The answer came unexpectedly. Apparently the house was well known in parapsychology circles. One day Larry received a visit from Fritz F., a noted "ghost hunter." Fritz had visited the house many times over the years when it had stood empty. He had even written about it in one of his many books. Now, it seemed, he wished to see if there were any changes in the evil emanations due to the house's occupancy. Larry told him how the house was affecting Eunice and, as he now realized, himself.

Fritz F. saw that the time for investigation and observation was over. This was now the time for purification. He told Larry briefly of the power of Chant-O-Matics and offered to purify the house for him.

The ritual was brief and, as Larry commented, simple.

"Don't let the simplicity fool you," said Fritz, with a smile. "It's the most effective thing I know."

As if to verify what he said, Eunice started humming happily to herself as she moved around the room. Color seemed to have already come back to her cheeks.

The baby was born and soon was gurgling happily in the brightly painted nursery. Less than a year later, when Larry's job dictated that they move to another town, the couple were ecstatic to find that their now beautifully cared-for house sold for $85,000!

How Jane M. Got Her First Good Night's Sleep in Years, After Chant-O-Matics Had Miraculously Purified Her

▶ Although Jane M. was obviously not possessed, she undoubtedly did behave at times as though she were con-

trolled by an evil being. She could be extremely vindictive, petty, spiteful, and selfish. She could never keep
any friends and even her long-suffering brother, Frank,
was hard put to it to excuse her many actions. Yet he
loved his sister dearly and refused to lose faith in her.

Jane, for her part, seemed truly contrite after any of her
vindictive actions. She could never sleep well at night,
feeling remorse for some act she had done during the
day. Her face grew white and drawn, with dark rings
under the eyes. No matter how angry Frank had felt at
the time of any one of Jane's actions, he could not but
help feel sorry for her when he saw her white face the following morning.

It was Jane herself who finally asked for help. Realizing
that she was destroying herself, that even her only friend,
Frank, must eventually be repelled by her actions, she
pleaded with him to purify her somehow of the evil within
her. Frank could not ignore her request.

Frank did a Chant-O-Matic ritual without even telling Jane
he was going to do it. Although from past experience he
had every faith in the power of the chant, he wanted to
be absolutely sure that the results would not just be due to
the power of suggestion. He need not have worried. The
following morning Jane greeted him "bright-eyed and
bushy-tailed." She guessed at once what he had done
and threw her arms around her brother. It was the first
good night's sleep she had had in a very long time and
she sobbed her thanks, confident now that her evil self
was finally behind her.

How Betty I. Was Finally Able to Wear the Long-Cursed Family Heirloom

▶ The beautiful pendant necklace had been in Betty I.'s family for many years. It had belonged to her mother, her grandmother and, before that, her great-grandmother. The necklace, an intricate design of turquoise stones set in solid gold, had seldom been worn by any of the women, however. It was believed to be cursed.

Betty's great-grandfather, an archaeologist, had brought the necklace back from Egypt. The story was that it had been stolen from a Pharaoh's tomb and was therefore forever cursed by the ancient Egyptian deities! There certainly seemed to be some substance to the story for whenever one of the family women wore the beautiful jewel, she would fall sick with an abnormally high fever that the doctors could not diagnose.

Betty loved the necklace. Its beauty had fascinated her since she first saw it as a little girl. She was determined to find a way to wear it without suffering the effects of the curse. She delved into all the books she could find on ancient Egypt and its magic, including all her great-grandfather's old books and excavation notes. To no avail. Far from finding an antidote, she could not even pinpoint the original owner nor the origin of the curse.

She tried wearing the necklace one more time, hoping that perhaps it was all pure superstitious nonsense. Unfailingly she fell ill and her husband, Paul, went nearly frantic with worry. It was her doctor who offered a solution.

"I don't know about this particular necklace," he said, examining it closely, "but I'm willing to bet that Chant-O-Matics can purify just about anything."

He told Betty of the power of the chant and took the time to write out for her a chant "to purify an object."

The chant worked beautifully. As soon as she had finished the ritual, Betty, just a little hesitantly, put the pendant around her neck and fastened the clasp. She waited. Nothing happened. She wore the necklace all that day and all the next. She felt a little silly walking about the house in jeans and a sweater wearing such an elaborate piece of jewelry, but she proved her point. The curse had been removed!

19

YOU CAN USE CHANT TO PROTECT YOURSELF FROM HARASSMENT

*I*n today's world of Hard Sell, the name of the game, from the point of view of the vendor, seems to be harassment. If you harass a potential customer hard enough and long enough, he or she will eventually tire and give in to you. This certainly seems to be today's philosophy.

YOU DON'T HAVE TO BE PLAGUED BY SALESPEOPLE

Why should you be subjected to such pressure? Why should you have to put up with this bombardment that has no end? Most people have no alternative. They get flyers through the mail; telemarketers incessantly call; they are surrounded by circulars and advertisements.

But, thanks to Chant-O-Matics, you can be rid of all this. You can live peacefully and undisturbed, happy in the knowledge that salespeople and telemarketers will be passing you by, not daring to break in upon you.

IT'S NOT HARD TO SAY "NO"

There are many people who just cannot say "No." No matter how much they dislike a person or a product, they feel that if they give in quickly, then everything will be over and there will be no more conflict. They dearly wish they could reject the sales pitch, but, unfortunately, they cannot . . . or so they believe.

In actual fact, through the power of the chant, you *can* reject what you do not desire. You *can* send a salesperson packing. By the simple action of repeating one of the chants given below, you can have the strength to be your own master; to decide for yourself what you do or do not want.

THEY WON'T TAKE YOU TO COURT!

You can even protect yourself from legal harassment, through the power of the chant! I am not suggesting that you give up paying your bills and chant your way through any and all indebtedness! But should the occasion arise where you are behind in some payments and, temporarily, unable to meet your obligations, do not panic when you are threatened with court action. You can, here, ensure that such action does not come about by using Chant-O-Matics.

FIVE CHANTS TO PROTECT YOU FROM MONETARY HARASSMENT

These chants may be done any day of the week.
Light candles and incense.
Sit, stand, or kneel and chant:

1 Sum welig man wais; ...

2 Mud twine and daighwam lees; ...

3 Ond him nan monn ne seeld; ...

4 Gemiltsa me, ond send; ...

5 Eala sunu gethenk god; ...

FIVE CHANTS TO PROTECT YOU FROM LEGAL PROCEEDINGS

These chants may be done any day of the week.
Light candles and incense.
Sit, stand, or kneel and chant:

1 Faedar ic bidde thay hait; ...

2 Sum mann ferde fram; ...

3 Tha gebryde hit thate; ...

4 Da ferde sum weard; ...

5 Ond brohte otherum to; ...

FIVE CHANTS FOR THE EXPULSION OF UNWANTED VISITORS

These chants may be done any day of the week.
Light candles and incense.
Sit, stand, or kneel and chant:

1 Nat ik hwait besorgad; ...

2 Gedafenad, gedafenad, gedafenad beo; ...

3 Ealle menn heriad; ...

4 Dohtor welwillendnesse; ...

5 Thone wast giet nast; ...

How Earl T. Brought an End to Threats of Legal Action, Through Chant

▶ Earl T., foolishly, had been talked into signing a contract for a set of encyclopedias that he really had no great interest in and that he would probably never in his life use. The salesperson had been very persuasive, to say the least. For some months Earl had struggled to make the payments, but it stretched his skimpy budget beyond its limit. He began to fall further and further behind in the payments.

To start with, the company seemed very understanding. They sent Earl reminders to make the payments. Some of them were quite cute in the wording, and even had little cartoon characters looking bewildered because they hadn't heard from him! Earl didn't feel too bad.

But then the tone suddenly changed: Earl had written to explain his position, but apparently the company computer was not interested. No more little cartoon characters appeared. In their place was the name and address of a collection agency. Apparently unaware that Earl could not find the single monthly payments, they demanded the full outstanding balance. When they threatened to take legal action, Earl really panicked.

His good friend Chuck finally calmed Earl. Chuck was a book-club fanatic and though he had no financial problems, Chuck knew the problems of meeting payments on time. He had even had a run-in with a billing computer.

One of Chuck's more recent book-club acquisitions was a book on Chant-O-Matics. From this he gave Earl a simple ritual to do to protect him from legal proceedings.

Earl did the ritual and waited. He had a long wait, for nothing more came from the collection agency! Not a single word! His "deadline" came and went, but nothing happened. In time, and to finally ease his conscience, Earl paid off his debt and even came to read and enjoy the encyclopedias.

How Eileen B., Who Could Never Say "No," Used Chant-O-Matics to Stop Being Tempted!

▶ Eileen B. had the best-equipped kitchen in her neighborhood. She had every modern gadget, every latest improvement in pots and pans, matched sets of dishes and cutlery, and closets full of detergents, dishwashers, sponges, mops, etc. It wasn't that she loved cooking or any sort of housework; it was simply that she could never say "No" to a salesperson, or even to a sales circular!

Eileen's husband tore his hair! She was forever asking for extra food money because she had blown her budget on some new gadget she had seen demonstrated. He couldn't deny her the money, and he certainly couldn't stay home to ride rein on her. He pleaded with Eileen, but he knew only too well how weak she was where salespeople were concerned.

It was after much searching and consultation with his associates that Eileen's husband finally came into contact with Chant-O-Matics. Excitedly he rushed home and, as he suspected, had no trouble in "selling" Eileen on the idea of using them to strengthen her resistance.

It was a day to be marked on the calendar for Eileen when, the very morning following her doing the ritual, an "Avon Lady" called to tempt her. Eileen felt an inner glow as she firmly, but politely, said "No, thank you!"

20

PROTECT YOUR HOME AND FAMILY WITH THE ALL-ENVELOPING COVER OF CHANT-O-MATICS

YOUR HOME IS YOUR CASTLE

There was a time when your home was indeed your castle; when you could just pull up the drawbridge and close out anything or anyone you considered undesirable. You could protect yourself and your family from attack by death, disaster, and disease. Today most people can no longer do this. Their only protection is in the form of life insurance and health insurance—in effect, anticipatory cure and recompense rather than prevention.

You do not have to be like others. You can still have your drawbridge to guard yourself and your family. Chant-O-Matics is that drawbridge. Through the power of the chant you can ensure that you are safe from accident, safe from disease, protected from impending disaster. Safe from death? Well, see the case of Charlie D., detailed at the end of this chapter, and judge for yourself!

YOU ARE MASTER OF YOUR HOUSE

As a master of Chant-O-Matics, you are automatically master of your house. Though your family is away from home, you can still watch over them and guard them. Protection is as easy as saying a few simple words. As with all the chants given in this book, you *must feel*, strongly, the meaning of the words when you say them. You must put yourself into chant. But when it comes to protecting your home and family, I am sure such feeling goes without saying.

THROUGH CHANT-O-MATICS YOU NEED NEVER FEAR

Tempest, tornado, storm, lightning, car crash, train wreck . . . the list of words of tragedy that strike fear—if not terror—into the hearts of the majority need leave you unaffected. You have the power to protect yourself and your loved ones from any and all of the above. What tragedy is there that can touch you? With Chant-O-Matics, the answer must be "none"!

FIVE CHANTS TO PROTECT YOURSELF

These chants may be done any day of the week.
Light candles and incense.
Sit, stand, or kneel and chant:

1 Brengan theekan; ...

2 Kweckan sininge leofa; ...

3 Eallum thearl licode; ...

4 Astyrian ongonn mid songe; ...

5 Kwen lair lufiend beon; ...

FIVE CHANTS TO PROTECT YOUR FAMILY

These chants may be done any day of the week.
Light candles and incense.
Sit, stand, or kneel and chant.

1 Hwaet is theet ge may; ...

2 Nim nu da nam gewritu; ...

3 Licre tide dohtor biddenne; ...

4 Gewendon hie ham mid; ...

5 Ik smeed, minre heo; ... ...

FIVE CHANTS TO PROTECT YOUR HOME

These chants may be done on any day of the week.
Light candles and incense.
Sit, stand, or kneel and chant:

1 Geendung ealles fleeskes com; ...

2 Tha on tham eetooan; ...

3 Thate weeter wais fiftyne; ...

4 Buton tham anum; ...

5 Sevill Iraey not; ...

How Jerry F.'s House and Family Alone Survived the Tornado Through the Use of the Protection Chant

▶ Unless you have been through a tornado, have lived in its path and watched its inevitable approach, you cannot know the fear it can instill. You may hear reports of the devastation it has wrought along its path . . . the path that now leads to you. All you can do, it seems, is pray.

Jerry F., his wife, and two small children lived in Kentucky. They had learned to live with the threat of tornadoes over the years. They had heard reports of them. They had visited towns and villages that had been destroyed by them. They had even seen a tornado in the distance, leading away from them. They had never, though, actually been in the unenviable position of seeing the monstrous dark column advancing on them. Never, that is, until recently. Then their turn came.

The size of the column was the thing that most impressed Jerry. It was huge, towering up into the skies above the little southern town and stretching across, many hundreds of yards in diameter. It advanced toward them with the speed of an express train. Herding his family into the basement,

Jerry crouched with them, listening to the whimpering of his daughters, scarcely audible over the roar of the approaching monster. What could he do to save them? How could he protect them?

In the few short minutes before the tornado struck, Jerry remembered the power of Chant-O-Matics. His book of chants lay on the dresser beside his bed, in the room above them. Never had he run so fast. He dashed up the stairs as fast as he could, grabbed the book, and dashed down again. Flicking through the pages he found what he wanted, a chant of protection. With his wife's hands held in his, he began the chant, putting his whole being into it.

The tornado struck the town and passed on. Devastation lay all around. Buildings were flattened and people were injured. But Jerry F. and his family emerged, unscathed, to find theirs to be the only house standing for many blocks around.

How Peggy P., a Newcomer to Chant, Ensured Her Daughter's Safety in a Disastrous School-Bus Crash

Peggy P. had long had an ominous premonition that one day there would be a terrible accident at the gateless railroad crossing just outside the New Jersey village where she lived. She didn't know why she felt there would be such an accident; certainly the trains that ran along that line were few and far between. The exact nature of the accident she did not know, yet she knew it would be a major disaster.

A neighbor was one day telling Peggy about Chant-O-Matics. Fascinated, Peggy asked if they could be used to protect when it was felt there was just the possibility of danger.

"Of course," said her friend. "In fact Chant-O-Matics is often used that way. You'd be surprised the sense of security it can give you to know that, by this simple process, you can protect your family so well from any danger that might threaten."

Peggy was impressed and decided to try it herself. She did the chant her neighbor suggested and, sure enough, felt a great peace of mind. How thankful she was that she had done it, when, less than a week later, at the unguarded railroad-crossing, a freight train hit a school-bus full of children returning from a day's outing. Peggy's daughter was on that bus. Of the 40 children on the bus, 28, together with the bus driver, were killed. Peggy's daughter was actually the only one to escape without any injury of any sort.

How Charlie D. Fell 8,000 Feet Without a Parachute—and Lived!

▶ Charlie D. had always been known as "Lucky Charlie," but luck had nothing to do with his ultimate triumph over Fate. Charlie was a light-plane enthusiast. He loved to fly. He did not have a pilot's license himself, but was always able to beg rides with his many friends at the local airport. He especially loved to go up in his friend Dean's old open-cockpit Waco biplane. He swore there was no thrill like that of feeling the slipstream blowing in your face as you leaned out of the cockpit.

Something of a "Walter Mitty," Charlie would fantasize as he sat in the forward cockpit, seeing himself alternately as a WWI flying ace and as a daring Air Show wing-walker. As the latter, he would imagine himself clawing his way across, from strut to strut, between the wings. Dean, knowing of Charlie's fantasies, would loop and roll the old plane, throwing it around the sky, as a fighter ace or a flying-circus pilot would do.

It was one, beautiful, clear, summer day that Charlie got his biggest thrill—and decided to fly no more in the old Waco! He and Dean had taken off, as usual, in the early morning and climbed to a safe height for performing aerobatics. It was seldom that either of them bothered to wear a parachute, though they never failed to strap themselves tightly in. Exactly what happened that morning no one knows; not even Charley. It may have been that he had been dreaming, once again, of climbing out onto the wing. Anyway, for whatever reason he had unbuckled his seat belt. About this same time Dean started a loop, but halfway through changed his mind and flipped the plane into a roll. The flip sent Charlie speeding out of the cockpit and flying—without plane and without parachute!

In a split second Charlie snapped out of his dream-world and back to reality. Reality was that he was heading for the ground at an ever-increasing speed! He later denied that his whole past life flashed before him. What did flash before him, however, was the page of a book he had recently been studying. It was a page of Chant-O-Matics and the chant was one to protect yourself.

"It was as though the page itself was right there in front of me," he said. "All I did was read it off—and, boy! did I put some feeling into it!" Charlie plummeted down slightly to one side of the county airport. He momentarily blacked out, which may have been a contributing factor to his survival, for it ensured the complete limpness of his body. He hit, and crashed through the outer tips of the branches of a high tree. From there he went into dense bushes and accumulated mulch over slightly boggy ground.

By the time Dean had landed the plane and then arrived, panic-stricken, with a number of fellow aviators, Charlie was sitting up checking his bones to see if anything was broken. Miraculously nothing was. Later medical examination showed that the only change in Charlie was that he was one-and-one-half inches shorter! It was a very long time before he again ventured up into the sky.

21

THE CHANT—
YESTERDAY, TODAY,
AND TOMORROW

EMOTIONAL CONTROL

Words are, in themselves, a means to emotional control over persons and events. How effectively they control is dependent upon the speaker. It was a chant, or spell, that first brought to Man the feeling that he was able to exercise supernatural abilities with the minimum of danger to himself. The foundation of successful casting of spells lies in the power and mystery of "the word." It is even believed that some words are in themselves so powerful that they are impossible to speak disparagingly. They may only be used on certain very special occasions.

Eliphas Levi, the French magician, said, "In magic to have said is to have done; to affirm and will what ought to be, is to create." Of course, two necessary ingredients are needed. They are a strong belief/desire, willing that it be so, and the right words. Finding the right words is usually a question either of trial and error, or of finding previously effective (time-tested) words. A good example of the latter is the Lord's Prayer, used to accomplish magical ends for centuries—everything from removing warts to removing demons!

RHYTHM AND RHYME

Another ingredient mentioned by some magicians is rhythm. Chants and spells should either rhyme or be repetitive with a heavy sonorous beat. This contributes to a gradually rising state of excitement within the chanter him-herself, adding immeasurably to the power produced. And here can be found an interesting point: Many of today's successful rock songs feature repetition of a word or phrase, often repeated over and over again. Could this be a contributory factor to the success of those singers? I think so.

WORLD CREATED
WITH A WORD

The Anglo-Saxon word *spel* means "a saying," a form of words. From this, of course, we get our word "spell," of which the chant is a form. ("Chant" itself is derived from the Latin *cantare:* to sing.) The concept of a spell/chant appears to have come from the idea that there is a connection between words and the things they signify. It is said that all things are in sympathy and therefore act and react upon one another, even after actual contact is broken.

According to the First Book of Moses *(Genesis)*. God created the world with *words:*

> And God said, "Let there be light:" and there was light. . . . And God said, "Let there be a firmament in the midst of the waters. . . . ." And God said, "Let the waters under the heaven be gathered together unto one place, and let the dry land appear. . . . And God said, "Let the earth bring forth grass. . . ."

Here is the perfect example of the constructive power of words. And this power that God used in creating the World—the Power of the Word—was believed to be a power that could also be acquired by Man. Chants and incantations are the earliest forms of magic known and can be found recorded on cuneiform tablets dating back over five thousand years.

Among the Sumerian and Babylonian peoples, it was generally believed that sickness was caused by evil spirits entering the body. For a sick person to be cured, a magician would have to draw out these spirits by the use of magical chants. Such incantation was usually accompanied by the burning of incense. The ancient thought was that the smoke of the incense carried the words up to the gods.

THE MYSTERIOUS POWER
OF THE MANTRA

In all ages and all places there has been this idea of, this belief in, the power of certain sounds, words, or phrases.

> Galen writeth, that a certain Sorcerer, by uttering and muttering but one word, immediately killed, or caused to die, a serpent or scorpion; Benivenius in his book *De Abd. morb. Caus.*, affirmeth, that some kind of people have been observed to do hurt, and to surprise others, by using certaine sacred and holy words.
>
> *Tryall of Witch-craft*, London, 1616

We all remember "Open Sesame" from the story of Ali Baba. And, of course, the all-powerful "Abracadabra," still used by stage conjurers today. In the East especially, this belief in the power of words and sounds has been built into a great philosophy. It is a system embraced by certain Hindus and Buddhists and termed "Mantra Yoga."

The *mantra* can come about in several ways. It might be a single word, or a whole phrase, that has come from inspiration through meditation. Or it might be a carefully-plotted distillation, or reduction, from a large volume or holy book. In this latter method, a section of the holy book is paraphrased and compressed to its main essentials, perhaps only a paragraph or two in length. This, in turn, is then brought down to a single sentence or even a single word. It would then be thought that the resultant phrase or word would still contain all of the main essentials, all the magical power, of the original whole. Repetition of this word or phrase produces the necessary vibrations to accomplish what is desired. This is a belief, and a practice, becoming more and more popular today. In Transcendental Meditation™ a *mantra* is used to bring about a sense of well-being, relaxation, good health, etc. So, in many of the Chant-O-Matics in this book, the mantric form has been employed.

THE POWER
OF THE SPOKEN WORD

The power of the spoken word is implicity believed in, especially if emanating from a known expert of the magical art, and even more so if in an unknown or uncommon language. Thus, the magicians of Ancient Egypt used foreign words for their chants. Herodotus, the oldest Greek historian whose words have come down to use, tells that magical chanting by the Egyptian magicians was what enabled them to lift the great blocks with which they built the pyramids.

The magicians of the Middle Ages also used foreign languages, as did the medicine men of the American Indians and the various magical/religious leaders of many, many groups down to the present day. It is interesting to note that the Ecumenical Council, in 1983, only voted to allow the Mass to be said in languages other than Latin if the Latin was retained for "the precise verbal formula which is essential to the sacrament," i.e., the words that are spoken by the priest to transform the bread and wine into the Body and Blood.

CHANT-O-MATICS: YOUR POWER OF THE FUTURE

We can see, then, that magical words in the form of chants have been used throughout the ages, and used effectively. Chant-O-Matics is a continuation of this honorable tradition and is a way of allowing YOU to follow in the footsteps of such notables as Dr. John Dee, Eliphas Levi, Cornelius Agrippa, St. Thomas Aquinas, Madame Blavatsky, and a host of others. Chant-O-Matics is the magic of the future. It is *your* magic; enabling you to do and to have what you desire. Take it, and use it well.

INDEX

A

Altar, 5-6
  height of, 6
Antiques:
  chants to find, 68-69
    example of, 73
Appearance, 6-7
Artifacts:
chants to find, 68-69
example of, 73
Attraction, *See* Love/attraction
    chants
Aura, 157
reinforcing, chants for, 159-60

B

Bedwetting, using chants to stop,
  129
Better job:
  chants for, 37-39
    example of, 39-40
Better living, chants for, 147
Black Magic, 155-56
Book of Sacred Magic of Abra-
    Melin the Mage, The, 3-4
Breaking up undesirable friendships:
  chants for, 87-93
    example of, 92-93
Broken limb, chants to mend, 140

C

Calming chants, 131-36
  to calm/soothe the nerves,
    133-34

examples of, 134-36
to prepare you for an unsettling
    situation, 134
relaxation, 132-33
Candles, 6
Card playing, chants for, 21-23
Ceremonial Magicians, vi-vii, 7
Chant-O-matic workshop, 1-11
  dress/appearance, 6-7
  furnishing, 5-6
  joy of simplicity, 4-5
  location, 5
Chant-O-matical simplicity, 4-5
Chant-O-matics, using to obtain a
    Chant-O-matic workshop,
    7-8
Chants:
  automatic attainment through,
    ix
  for a better job, 37-39
  to bring about a decision in your
    favor, 98
    example of, 99-100
  to bring about full recovery, 141
  to bring money to another,
    58-60
    example of, 61-62
  to bring pressure to bear on
    another, 97-98
    example of, 102-3
  to calm/soothe the nerves,
    133-34
  as catalysts, viii
  choosing, 10-11
  for a circle of protection, 158-59

Printed in the United States
by Baker & Taylor Publisher Services